THE Popinjays

By the same author

THE HOLLOW CROWNS
A History of the Battles of the Wars of the Roses

THE DECEIVERS
The Solution to the Murder of the Princes in the Tower

THE LORDLY ONES
A History of the Neville Family and their part in the Wars of the Roses

The Popinjays

Popinjay: *1. A person given to vain displays and empty chatter;*

   2. A coxcomb.

**[Random House Dictionary of
the English Language]**

   3. A type of vanity or empty conceit.

[Oxford English Dictionary]

*A History of the Woodville family and an account
of their involvement in English History during the
Late Medieval Age.*

GEOFFREY RICHARDSON

This edition published 2000

by Baildon Books
P.O. Box 107, SHIPLEY, W. Yorks BD17 6UR

Printed in Great Britain by
Pennine Printing Services Ltd.
Ripponden, West Yorkshire, England

ISBN 09527621 3 7

This one has to be for two ladies –
fellow Ricardians both – without whose help
The Popinjays might never have seen
the light of day.
It is for Pam Benstead of Kempsey, Worcester,
"who is much too young to be my Editor",
and for Judy Pimental of Alameda, California,
who supplied initial research material
in generous quantities.
And, it is, as always, for a third lady –
my dearest wife, Betty.

CONTENTS

Illustrations   9

Pedigree of The Woodvilles   10/11

Introduction   12

Chapter

ONE   *"Oh Lancaster, I fear thy overthrow..."*   15

TWO   *"... The handsomest man in England ..."*   21

THREE   *"...Warwick rated him and said his father was but a squire ... and since then himself made by marriage..."*   27

FOUR   *"... My title's good, and better far than his ..."*   35

FIVE   *"...One way or other, she is for a king; and she shall be my love, or else my queen ..."*   39

SIX   *"... to know his meaning, they asked him, smiling, with whom he wished to ally himself, and he replied, the daughter of Lord Rivers ..."*   43

SEVEN   *"Alas poor Clarence! Is it for a wife that thou art malcontent? I will provide thee ..."*   49

EIGHT   *"... So we, well-cover'd with the night's black mantle ... may beat down Edward's guard and seize himself ..."*   55

NINE   *"... the people ... seeing their king detained as a prisoner, refused to take any notice of proclamations ..."*   59

TEN   *"... the queen persevered for fifteen days ere she would anything intend to the said treaty of marriage ..."*   65

ELEVEN   *"... I like not this flight of Edward's; for doubtless Burgundy will yield him help And we shall have more wars before 't be long ..."*   71

TWELVE   *"... Sound drums and trumpets. Farewell sour annoy! for here, I hope, begins our lasting joy ..."*   77

THIRTEEN   *"... the king ... took to his bed about Easter time and on 9 April gave up his spirit to his Maker at ... Westminster ... in 1483 ..."*   85

FOURTEEN   *"We are so important, that even without the king's uncle we can make and enforce these decisions."*   91

FIFTEEN   *"Thus fell Hastings, killed not by those enemies he had always feared, but by a friend whom he had never doubted."*   97

SIXTEEN   *"... Bounden am I, And that greatly, To be content. Seeing plainly Fortune doth wry. All contrary From mine intent ..."*   101

SEVENTEEN   *"... Ah, my poor princes! ah, my tender babes! My unblown flowers, new-appearing sweets ..."*   107

EIGHTEEN   *"... The Countess began to hope well of her son's fortunes, supposing the deed would prove for the profit of the Commonwealth ..."*   113

NINETEEN   *"... the King ... in the presence of the Mayor and Citizens of London, made the said denial in a loud and clear voice ..."*   118

TWENTY   *"... We will unite the white rose and the red. Smile heaven upon this fair conjunction ..."*   123

TWENTY ONE   *"... then, in a moment see How soon this mightiness meets misery, And if you can be merry then. I'll say a man may weep upon his wedding-day ..."*   129

TWENTY TWO   *"... Last scene of all, That ends this strange eventful history ..."*   137

Epilogue   *"... last of the Popinjays ..."*   142

Acknowledgements   145

Sources   146

Index   147

Illustrations

Edward IV	14
Richard Woodville, First Earl Rivers	26
Jacquetta of Luxembourg, Duchess of Bedford	28
Richard Neville, Earl of Warwick, "Kingmaker"	34
Elizabeth Woodville, Queen of England	44
Royal Seal of Elizabeth Woodville	48
Louis XI of France	67
The Earl of Warwick in full plate armour	70
Elizabeth Woodville	76
Anthony Woodville, 2nd Earl Rivers	84
Richard III	90
Henry Stafford, 2nd Duke of Buckingham	106
Margaret Beaufort	112
Sir William Catesby	117
Sheriff Hutton Castle	122
Henry VII	128
Mary Tudor and Charles Brandon	131
Lady Jane Grey	135
Protector Somerset	136
John Dudley, Duke of Northumberland	143

The Portraits of Richard III and Henry VII are reproduced by kind permission of the Society of Antiquaries of London.

All other illustrations, Coats of Arms and signatures are provided by Geoffrey Wheeler of London.

The Pedigree of the Woodvilles

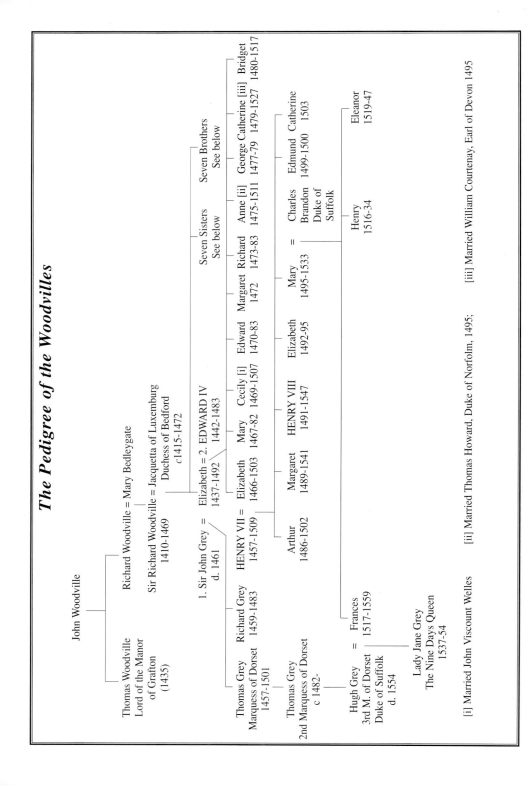

John Woodville

Thomas Woodville Lord of the Manor of Grafton (1435)

Richard Woodville = Mary Bedleygate

Sir Richard Woodville = Jacquetta of Luxemburg
1410-1469   Duchess of Bedford
c1415-1472

Elizabeth = 2. EDWARD IV
1437-1492   1442-1483

Seven Sisters
See below

Seven Brothers
See below

1. Sir John Grey =
d. 1461

HENRY VII =
1457-1509

Elizabeth
1466-1503

Mary
1467-82

Cecily [i]
1469-1507

Edward
1470-83

Margaret
1472

Richard
1473-83

Anne [ii]
1475-1511

George
1477-79

Catherine [iii]
1479-1527

Bridget
1480-1517

Thomas Grey Marquess of Dorset 1457-1501

Richard Grey
1459-1483

Arthur
1486-1502

Margaret
1489-1541

HENRY VIII
1491-1547

Elizabeth
1492-95

Mary
1495-1533

= Charles Brandon Duke of Suffolk

Edmund
1499-1500

Catherine
1503

Thomas Grey 2nd Marquess of Dorset c 1482-

Henry
1516-34

Eleanor
1519-47

Hugh Grey 3rd M. of Dorset Duke of Suffolk d. 1554

= Frances
1517-1559

Lady Jane Grey
The Nine Days Queen
1537-54

[i] Married John Viscount Welles   [ii] Married Thomas Howard, Duke of Norfolm, 1495;   [iii] Married William Courtenay, Earl of Devon 1495

SISTERS OF ELIZABETH WOODVILLE

1. Margaret, m. Thomas Maltravers, heir to Earl of Arundel. d. 1491

2. Anne, m. [1] William Bourchier, heir to Earl of Essex;
   [2] George Grey. Earl of Kent.
   d. 1489

3. Jacquetta, m. Lord Strange of Knockyn.
   d. 1481

4. Joan, m. Lord Grey of Ruthyn.
   d. 1490

5. Katherine, m.   [1] Henry Stafford, 2nd Duke of Buckingham;
   [2] Jasper Tudor, Duke of Bedford;
   [3] Sir Richard Wingfield.
   d. 1512

6. Mary, m. William Herbert, 2nd Earl of Pembroke.
   d. 1481.

7. Martha, m. Sir John Bromley of Hextall in Shropshire.
   d. unknown.

BROTHERS OF ELIZABETH WOODVILLE

1. Anthony, Lord Scales, 2nd Earl Rivers, executed 1483

2. Sir John Woodville, executed 1469

3. Lionel, Bishop of Salisbury. d. 1484

4. Sir Edward Woodville, k. in battle 1488

5. Richard, 3rd and last Earl Rivers. d. 1491

6. Lewis, died young.

7. John, died young.

Introduction

The Wars of the Roses were so named, centuries after they had ended, by an eminent Scots' historical novelist with a fine turn of phrase. They lasted for some 30 years from May 1455 to August 1485. They were not an unbroken conflict, comprising in all fourteen battles - some say fifteen - with assorted skirmishes in between, and the main cluster of actions, six of them, taking place between July 1460 and the end of March, 1461.

The Wars were fought between opposing branches of the Plantagenet dynasty, which ruled England - and much of France - for 300 years. When the first battle was fought, at St Albans on May 22nd 1455, the leader of the senior branch was Richard, Duke of York, then aged 44 years. York was married to Cecily Neville, the Rose of Raby, youngest daughter of Ralph, first Earl of Westmorland and his Countess, Joan Beaufort, who was descended directly from Edward III via his third surviving son, John of Gaunt, Duke of Lancaster. Through his marriage, York enjoyed the support of his powerful in-laws, the Nevilles of Middleham, led by Richard, Earl of Salisbury and his eldest son, another Richard, Earl of Warwick.

The nominal leader of the House of Lancaster was the reigning King, Henry VI, who had succeeded to the throne in the first year of his life. In adulthood Henry had become prone to regular fits of melancholia which necessitated the appointment of a Protector - the Duke of York - to lead the King's Council until the King was well enough to resume power. However, Henry was not a strong ruler and Lancaster's real power lay in the hands of Henry's Queen, Margaret of Anjou and her clique of favourites, led by Edmund Beaufort, Duke of Somerset.

The Beauforts played a prominent role in the governance of England throughout Henry VI's reign and, like the Queen, they envied York his wealth [he was the richest man in England] and his status. Both Queen and Beauforts felt strong dislike, contempt even, for the Nevilles whom they regarded as parvenu upstarts trading on their distant royal links and wealthy only through marriage. For their part, York, Salisbury and Warwick fully reciprocated the dislike of their Lancastrian rivals. When the Hundred Years War for France was finally lost at Castillon in 1453, largely due to the lack of financial support from the Lancastrian-controlled Council, the exchanges between the two parties grew steadily more heated. It became inevitable that their differences would be settled by force of arms, for which there were many archers and men-at-arms available who no longer had profitable employment in France.

The scene was set for a battle of Titans to determine who would rule in England and, perhaps again, in France. The remaining great Houses of Plantagenet: Lancaster, with their legitimised sprig, the Beauforts, and York with his powerful allies the Nevilles, would occupy centre-stage in the first years of the coming conflict with other paladins taking their places as they fell. York's sons, Edward and Richard, would take up the family's banner in their turn as would younger Beauforts and John de Vere, Earl of Oxford and ever-loyal Lancastrian. And most of them would die in battle, or by the executioner's axe, or simply worn out from years of striving. Great nobles living through - nay, creating even - great times and leaving deep marks on the pages of England's history.

And then, there was another family. Not of the nobility much less the blood-royal; not brave in battle or skilled in warfare; not brilliant schemers or shrewd planners; a family whose only attributes were good-looks, ambition, and persistence. And yet a line which would mingle its blood and entangle its fortunes inextricably with those of the great Houses, which would pledge its support to both sides and be constantly involved in the history-making events all around them, and which, in the end, would survive into a new Century and a New Age after the great ones were dead and gone. And, whose descendants would continue to let ambition outrun their abilities to their own, and to others' dire cost.

They were the Woodvilles and this is their story.

Edward IV

(Detail from the Royal Window, Canterbury Cathedral)

CHAPTER ONE

"Oh Lancaster, I fear thy overthrow..."
[Henry VI pt 3]

The great mass of men moved slowly southwest, away from York, passing through and around Tadcaster till they reached a wide ridge beyond the tiny village of Towton. It was the afternoon of Friday, March 27th, 1461 and it would take a full day to marshal the men into battle-order. Henry Beaufort, Duke of Somerset, entrusted at 24 with the command of the greatest army ever assembled in England, was conscious of the enormity of his responsibility and anxious lest the reported, rapidly-approaching host of York should suddenly pour over the darkening sky-line to his front and attack before his deployment was completed.

A quick council of war with his commanders: Northumberland and Devon, Earls both, Lords Dacre and John Neville and, fiercest of Lancaster's generals, Lord John Clifford, and it was agreed that the position was strong and the main army would deploy here. Clifford would take a force of his mounted archers and push forward towards the crossing of the River Aire, where the oncoming army of York, reported already at Pontefract, was most likely to pass over the only natural obstacle between the two armies and delay their passage at need. Meanwhile, the others would array their 40,000 men across the ridge above Towton dale and wait on the coming of King Edward IV, newly-crowned usurper of the throne of their rightful monarch, Henry VI.

King Henry, that peace-loving, prayerful monarch, was not with his army. He was 10 miles behind in the city of York, constantly on his knees to intercede with the Almighty for the success of his arms. With him - more surprisingly - was his Queen, the martial Margaret of Anjou, victor of Wakefield and Second St Albans, acceding to her husband's request that she should join him in prayer as the Lenten fast drew to its close She was content to leave the conduct of the coming battle to her generals, Somerset and Clifford, certain of the rightness of her cause and confident that the massive army she had assembled would be more than enough to deal with the threat from any force the so-called Yorkist King had been able to muster in his few short weeks on his stolen throne. Edward would charge to his death on

Lancaster's spears as his father and brother had done less than three months before and that would be the end of civil strife in the war-torn Kingdom.

As the short evening drew on, Lord Clifford's force had reached as far as the Aire-crossing at Ferrybridge without meeting the enemy and, having broken the wooden span, was settling for the night in positions concealed from any hostile force approaching the opposite bank. John Clifford expected that Edward's vanguard would reach him by early light on Saturday morning and prepared a warm reception for whichever well-hated Yorkist adversary should first reach his position. In the event, he was very pleased to see, in the forefront of the well-mounted force which approached the river in the dawn-light, the quarterings of the Nevilles' white cross and Montacute's scarlet lozenges - the scouting party was led by none other than Richard Neville, Earl of Warwick, mightiest Lord in the faction of York. Clifford wasted no time and signalled his men to fire on the stationary group on the other bank which broke up in disorder under the repeated volleys and, headed by their erstwhile proud leader, fled away down the road towards Pontefract. First blood to Lancaster and the triumphant archers cheered their commander to the echo. Clifford, satisfied with the outcome of the first brief clash, knew that stronger force would follow and re-settled his men into their watching positions.

Soon, the growing, murmuring rumble heralding the approach of a mighty army reached the listening ambuscade and the men tensed in anticipation of the next order to shoot. This time the approach was more cautious, with the heavy cavalry held back out of range and quick scurrying archers running from cover to cover on the approaches to the wrecked bridge. Volleys of arrows were exchanged and took some toll on both sides, but there was no major effort to force the crossing and Clifford continued to wait and wait for the young King to make his charge. He had killed the father and brother of Edward of York at Wakefield and was eager to add a further member of the usurping Plantaganets to his list of dead. Let the young war-leader come on - John Clifford would know how to deal with him, giant or no, victor at Northampton and Mortimer's Cross or no. The death of his own father at First St Albans still cried aloud for vengeance and Clifford could wait.

Blinded by his hatred of the House of York, Clifford waited overlong, his eyes fixed only on the army opposite and when a sudden alarm came from his right flank he was taken by surprise. Edward's manoeuvrings had decoyed

Clifford's attention and a strong flanking force, led by Warwick's uncle, Fauconberg, had moved a mile upstream to Castleford, crossed the river and then moved swiftly down again to charge the ambushers in flank and rear. As the uproar of their assault reached the waiting Edward, he ordered his van forward, into and across the river, and Clifford called his men to mount and gallop hard up the road through Elmet to Towton, with the news that Edward of York was come to join battle. Joining in the hard-riding retreat, Clifford was caught by an arrow in the neck from Fauconberg's pursuing archers. Mortally wounded, he was dead by the time his Cumbrians rejoined their main force now fully assembled across their selected position spanning the roads from Saxton and Ferrybridge, their line near a mile long and many ranks deep.

The Yorkist advance guard halted on another ridge directly opposite and 500 yards distant from the waiting host of Lancaster. As Edward led his main body to join them, he could see that the enemy's numbers were at least equal to his own, strong as his army was, and he still waited news on the progress of the division led by John Mowbray, Duke of Norfolk, which had been delayed by Mowbray's illness. The hour was late, the skies - still more wintry than spring-like - were darkening quickly and snow flurries blew in the strengthening westerly wind. Eager as Edward ever was to come to blows with the opposing force at the earliest opportunity, he judged that, for once, he would do better to wait on events and ordered his men to take up position facing the enemy, on the low ridge at the head of the dale, and to settle in their battle lines for the night. They would make their fight on the morrow, March 29th, Palm Sunday of 1461.

So, two great armies settled in their positions and tried to sleep through a bitterly cold night made worse by driving rain, sleet and snow, which, significantly, was swept by a strong wind from behind the Yorkist lines into the faces of their adversaries. Many supporters of the House of Lancaster would pay a heavy price for that particular quirk of fate when morning came again.

At first light, Somerset sent his Lords and sergeants to rouse the army. The men stood in their lines, shaking snow from their leather jacks and surcoats, stamping and slapping to restore circulation. The luckier ones ate the food-scraps carefully hoarded since leaving York two days before. Opposite, they could hear, and partly discern through the constant snow flurries, the army of York likewise readying itself for battle. Soon they saw the leading ranks move forward down the slope towards their position and Dacre, Neville and Northumberland sent archers to the front ready to make the initial response to the anticipated attack.

The wind blew more strongly, carrying stinging chips of snow and ice into the faces of the Lancastrian lines and suddenly filled with the more-lethal sting of arrow heads. Men dropped, screaming, kicking, dying and, under the furious urging of their commanders the archers of Lancaster sent flight after flight of missiles towards the Yorkist line in reply. Soon, their supply of arrows and bolts exhausted, the counter-fire died down and they were able to see that it had had little effect. The Yorkist volleys had been sharp but few, intended to draw their opponents' fire, and their archers had withdrawn quickly after loosing them. The increase in range coupled with the headwind had caused all the Lancastrian fire to fall short of its target and now, the Yorkist bowmen advanced again to use their enemies' spent projectiles as well as their own, and their steady, accurate fire caused heavy losses in the front ranks opposite.

With no possibility of replying to the galling barrage they faced, the Lancastrians had no option but to move forward. They left their strong position on the ridge, pushing as quickly as possible through Towton dale and started up the sharp incline towards the waiting, killing steel of the Yorkist line. Just before noon, the two lines met and the awful clangour of steel on steel rose louder and louder in the keening wind, drowning the cries of wounded and dying. Hour after hour the men of Lancaster fought to reach the flat ground at the top of the rise. The dead of both sides fell in heaps between the two lines, and men threw their erstwhile comrades aside to make room for more killing. Those tiring, or wounded, fell back to give way to comrades pressing through from the rear lines, thus gaining a little respite, and then pressing forward again in their turn to take up the fight.

The roar of battle was loudest round the centre of the Yorkist line, where the cream of Lancaster's chivalry urged their men forward to attack the giant figure of Edward Plantagenet, mighty, deadly, wielding his two-handed sword with murderous effect on all who came within his long-armed reach. And their efforts were unavailing and lethal for them; Neville - cousin to the Kingmaker - died leading his Scottish legions brought out of the Border country six months before by promises of rich loot; Harry Percy, Earl of

Northumberland, another with many Scots in his train also died in vain, and Lord Dacre, behind the main battle to confer with Somerset, removed his casque to communicate better, and took a crossbow bolt through the throat for his pains. The Yorkist centre stood firm on the rock of its warrior-King.

On the wings it was different. Here, painfully, at awful cost, the Lancastrians had gained the top of the slope and were slowly, slowly, pushing the Yorkist lines back and back. Edward's army was outnumbered, as Margaret of Anjou had surmised it would be, and his case was made worse by the continued absence of John Mowbray with his Norfolk men. As the first evening shadows lengthened, both sides sensed that the fight was nearly done, the Yorkists were being pressed back on their own lines, they had less and less room to wield their weapons, the sheer weight of numbers opposing them had worn their resistance to tatters. Without new help, York's cause was lost - despite all their King might do in the centre of their battle - and feeling the enemy yielding, the army of Lancaster pressed ever harder forcing the wings backwards and inwards.

And then relief came. From the extreme right flank of York's line, there was shouting and renewed clashing of weapons and armour. The Duke of Norfolk had arrived and his comparatively fresh men plunged at once into the fight, forcing the Lancastrian left down and off their hard-won heights, pressing them further round, bending their line back, across and behind their own centre. From the verge of victory, the Lancastrian troops were suddenly fighting for their very lives and Edward, the Yorkist Colossus, sensing that the decisive moment had arrived, redoubled his efforts in the centre, urging his men forward again, forcing the enemy centre back and down the blood-drenched slope into the confusion of their left wing, driving and trampling and killing. And the men of Lancaster who had fought bravely and hard and without mercy, for many hours, knew that they were beaten and turned away from the cruel steel of York to run - down, away, anywhere where they might find relief from wounds and exhaustion and death.

Tired beaten men will always take the easiest path away from the stricken field, usually the one that leads downhill, and this they did at Towton, rushing and sliding down the steep slopes - slippery with snow and ice and blood - of the ravine of the Cock Beck. Normally a tiny stream, the beck was in full spate. Filled to overflowing with snow-water and days of rain, there was no easy escape here for tired running men. Some scurried up and down the bank in panic, until the pursuing Yorkists caught them and ended it; others plunged boldly into the stream to force across it and, dragged down by their armour, sank and drowned. Eventually, enough had died thus horribly to form bridges across which their following comrades might follow to the brief safety of the further bank, before the pursuers - using the same passages - caught them in turn.

The pursuit and killing went on for much of the night and when a body-count was made on the orders of the victorious Edward it was found that 28,000 men had died, the majority being from the army that had followed the banners of Lancaster. This news Edward sent to his mother, Cecily Neville, waiting in London with her younger children around her, saying that soon they would all be together again and could feast and celebrate the greatest victory ever recorded in England. Meanwhile, he ordered the digging of great grave-pits for the speedy interment of the dead and, into one of these was cast the broken, naked body of a minor gentleman, who had paid the full price for his loyalty to the House of Lancaster. Now just another nameless corpse in a mass grave, he had been Sir John Grey and left a widow and two young sons fruitlessly waiting his return.

The widow's maiden name was Elizabeth Woodville and it would have been better for England and the House of Plantagenet if her husband had escaped Towton field unscathed and, as so many of his comrades did, made his peace with the all-conquering King Edward IV.

Arms of the Cliffords.
The checks alternate in gold and blue,
the crossband is in red.

CHAPTER TWO

"....The handsomest man in England...."

Lady Elizabeth Grey was the first-born child of Richard Woodville, whose family were lesser landed-gentry in Northampton. Their principal holding was the Manor of Grafton in that county, which they had held since the middle of the 12th century, on a payment of 25 shillings a year to the Abbot of Grestein. Some three hundred years later, the family had made little progress in terms of wealth or social standing, though an earlier Richard Woodville had served eight terms as High Sheriff of Northamptonshire during the reign of Edward III and had attended seven parliaments as one of the members from his county. His son, John, had similar distinction in the reign of Richard II and his grandson, Thomas, served likewise under Kings Henry IV, V and VI and had also bought the manorial rights to Grafton from William de la Pole, Earl of Suffolk, in 1435.

Elizabeth's grandfather was yet another Richard Woodville, younger brother to Thomas, now Lord of the Manor of Grafton, and he had been fortunate - or possibly, clever - enough to be taken into the service of Henry V and then that of Henry's brother John, Duke of Bedford. Having his fortune to seek, Richard had taken part in the expeditions to France and by 1420, was an esquire of the body to the King and held the Office of Seneschal of Normandy with Manorial holdings in Preaux and Dangu to support his status. Following the death of Henry V, Bedford was made Regent for the infant Henry VI and he made Woodville his personal Chamberlain and then Lieutenant of Calais, an Office he held for eight years, until 1435. Shortly after this, his childless older brother died and Richard inherited Grafton, took up residence there and died some six years later.

Long before this, Richard the elder had brought his son, Richard, to the royal notice and as a compliment to the Father and in recompense for his loyal service to Henry V and, particularly, to John of Bedford, the younger Woodville was included in a festive mass knighting by the child-King, Henry VI at Leicester on Whit Sunday, 1426. Ironically, in light of later events, the first recipient of the collective guerdon was Richard Plantagenet, Duke of

York, father-to-be of Edward IV and Richard III. Some six years later, Sir Richard Woodville had taken his father's old post as Chamberlain to John of Bedford. He attended his master - widowed in 1432 through the death of his wife, Anne of Burgundy - at his magnificent wedding in the Cathedral of Therouanne in the early Summer of 1433 to the lovely, 17 year old daughter of the Count of St Pol, Jacquetta of Luxembourg. Jacquetta's family claimed descent from a serpent-witch, Melusine, the water-nymph of Lusignan, and anyone seeing the beauty and attraction of Jacquetta could well have believed their assertion.

Bedford toured Normandy with his bride and thence to England, where many civic receptions were held in her honour and eventually visiting Paris at the end of 1434, where the Regent was received "almost as a God". Between making a wife half his age happy, overseeing the rule of England in his nephew's name, and his role as Generalissimo of the English forces in France, it is not surprising that Bedford, like his brother Henry before him, died, worn out before his time, in September 1435. Nor that his young wife should have formed an attachment for his Chamberlain - already noted as "the handsomest man in England" - who would have been always on hand to offer words - and perhaps more - of comfort during Jacquetta's enforced, regular periods of grass-widowhood.

As a very marriageable widow, Jaquetta was granted return of her dowry by Letters Patent of February 8th 1438, on condition that she did not remarry without the consent of her King, Henry VI. However, within a year she was begging forgiveness of King Henry for having taken "but late ago to Husband, your true liegeman...Richard Woodville, not having thereto your Royal license and assent...". There can be little doubt as to the reason for the bereft Duchess of Bedford marrying, in some haste, the handsomest - and presumably most proximate - Englishman, over the violent protests of her own family and at an eventual cost of a £1,000 fine paid to the King's treasury. This large sum appears to have been found by the King's uncle, Cardinal Beaufort, in exchange for certain desirable manors in Dorset, Somerset and Wiltshire, formerly the property of the Dowager Duchess of Bedford. As many others would learn in the course of time, the cost of marriage with a Woodville often came high, in treasure and in blood.

The official pardon for the misdeed of the young, handsome couple was dated October 24th 1437, which was fortuitous, since the first result of their fruitful union appeared in the very same year, though the exact timing is not known. However, with that initial "difficulty" out of the way, Richard Woodville lost little time in re-ingratiating himself with the King and his close advisers, the Beauforts. The early effectiveness of his efforts is seen in the grant of the Office of Chief Rider of the forest of Saucy, close to the family Manor of Grafton and by the Summer of 1439, he was accompanying John Beaufort, third Earl of Somerset, who was riding with the force led by John, Lord Talbot to relieve Meaux, the only town east of Paris still held by the English. The expedition was successful in resupplying the garrison, but could not bring on a general battle with the besiegers and eventually withdrew back to Rouen, leaving Meaux to surrender on terms a short time later.

In the Winter of the following year, Woodville was selected to run a course in the lists with the chamberlain of the Duke of Burgundy, a passage of arms which, barring mischance, usually carried little physical danger and, in any event, courses run before Henry VI were invariably cut short by the peace-loving monarch after two or three passes. In the Summer of 1441, Richard Woodville went to France again with a reinforcing army led by Richard Duke of York, whose mission was to assist Talbot to raise the siege of Pontoise and thereby ensure that the English garrison at this strongpoint, threatening St Denis and Paris itself, was fully maintained. In a marching/countermarching campaign, brilliantly orchestrated by Talbot, the English forces successfully drove off the besieging French army with little loss. Indeed, but for a dilatory march by the reinforcing troops, Talbot could well have trapped King Charles, with most of his force, against the Seine and conceivably brought the campaign to an abrupt close. Unfortunately the assisting forces may have been more used to the chivalric niceties of the lists than the speedy manoeuvring and hard action necessary in the actual field, and the opportunity was lost.

Following this failure, Sir Richard Woodville - now a Knight-Banneret and Captain of Alencon "in recognition of his good services in the French wars" - returned home again to Grafton and his adoring, passionate wife, and their growing family. The Woodvilles were ever-notable in particular character-attributes, the men for their uxoriousness, the women for their fertility, and both sexes for their good looks. Sir Richard was no exception, so that the loving couple's first child, Elizabeth, had been joined by sisters

Katherine and Margaret and the first-born son of the family, Anthony, had arrived while his father was assisting York in the abortive contribution to Talbot's French campaign. Sister Mary appeared in 1443, and another daughter, Jacquetta, in the following year, with the second son, John, arriving late in 1445, a year which had great significance in the furthering of Woodville fortunes and influence.

The year previously, William de la Pole, Earl of Suffolk, one of the chief leaders of the Peace Party in England had negotiated secretly with Charles of France for a two-year truce. This to be effectively guaranteed by the betrothal of Henry VI to Margaret, daughter of Rene, Count of Anjou and King of Jerusalem, who, despite the grand titles, was a landless pensioner of the French court. In the Spring of 1445 then, a select party of English nobles under Suffolk's leadership went to France and conducted the 16 year-old Margaret to her first landing in her adoptive country at Portsmouth. Included in the conducting group was Richard Woodville and his wife Jacquetta, who, as another beautiful and vivacious French woman, easily made friends with the slightly forlorn Angevin Princess, soon to become Queen of England.

Jacquetta of Luxembourg was certainly a force to be reckoned with at the court of Henry VI. As widow of the King's uncle, she out-ranked all other ladies with the exception of the Queen, and her family had existing links with Margaret's through the marriage of Jacquetta's sister, Isabelle, with Charles of Anjou. Thus the two ladies quickly became fast friends and Lady Jacquetta received many gifts, including valuable jewels, as earnests of the affection in which Queen Margaret held her countrywoman. Nor was her husband left out of the Queen's beneficence, for, on May 8th, 1448, Richard Woodville, Knight-Banneret, was created Baron Rivers. At last, after 300 years of largely-unsuccessful efforts to scale England's social ladder, the Woodville family could be said to have arrived.

Others, better-born by far than Woodville, had been less fortunate. The King's last-surviving uncle, Humphrey of Gloucester, youngest brother of Henry V, had fallen foul of the party led by Suffolk and Cardinal Beaufort and, following his arrest on trumped-up charges, early in 1447, had mysteriously died, by poison some whispered. Beaufort himself had died six weeks later, according to rumour again, of a fit during a bout of insanity brought on by guilt over Gloucester's death. The only remaining obstacle to Suffolk's hegemony at the court of King Henry was Richard, Duke of York, who, with Gloucester's death had become heir-apparent to the childless King.

But with the Queen's connivance, York was removed from the mainstream of English politics by effective exile to Ireland as Viceroy for 10 years from September 1447.

All-powerful with the Queen's backing and his weak King's anxious compliance with any and all of his wishes, Suffolk made himself Duke and conferred similar distinction on Edmund Beaufort, Marquess of Dorset, and another fervent supporter of what was rapidly becoming the "Queen's Party". Beaufort, as the second Duke of Somerset, would be a key instigator of the quarrel which has come down to us as the Wars of the Roses.

Somerset was sent to France in York's place as commander in Normandy but he had insufficient troops to hold the dukedom against the increasingly warlike Charles VII, thanks to Suffolk's money-saving policies and, by the end of 1449, it was clear that Normandy was lost to England. At the following January Parliament, Suffolk appeared before the Estates of the Kingdom and made a long speech justifying all his policies but had seriously misjudged the credulousness of his auditors who, four days later, issued a warrant for his arrest on charges of High Treason. In an effort to save him, King Henry issued an order of banishment, but, en route to Calais, his small transport was taken by the ship "Nicholas of the Tower" and Suffolk was despatched, without more ado, beheaded, according to reports, "with a rusty sword".

Suffolk's death, though welcome to most in England, left the country without any firm hand on the tiller of the ship of state and, by the middle of 1450, Kent was 'up' and 40,000 men marched on London under the leadership of one, Jack Cade. Cade is variously described as "tailor", "sheep-shearer" and spoke of himself as John Mortimer, claiming royal descent through the Yorkist line. The rebels were met at Sevenoaks by a weak army led by Sir Humphrey and William Stafford, with whose staff rode Richard Woodville, Lord Rivers, and after failing to disperse as ordered by the Staffords, Cade's men attacked and routed the royal troops, defeating them totally and killing the two generals. Rivers made good his escape and kept well clear of the following strife which ended days later when a better-organised force, led by the Duke of Buckingham and Lord Clifford, met the rebels in the south London streets, forced them to disperse and killed Cade.

Through his wife's influence with the Queen, Rivers came out of the affair very well and, though he did not get the Office of Constable of England as was first rumoured, he was admitted to the Order of the Garter and became a member of the King's Council. In October, he was named to command a force to be sent to Gascony to repel a renewed French invasion, but, as ever, funds were short to equip the necessary fleet and delays continued until news came that on June 30th, 1451, the French had taken Bordeaux and Rivers' expedition was abandoned.

In the next four years, Rivers spent much of his time in Calais where he had been appointed Lieutenant to the Captain of the port, Edmund Beaufort, Duke of Somerset. He was not involved in the fighting which effectively ended the Hundred Years War with France at Castillon in July 1453, nor was he at St Albans on the 22nd of May two years later, when Somerset and Clifford met their end in the first battle of the Wars of the Roses. He was still in Calais some months later, when the new Captain, Richard Neville, Earl of Warwick arrived to take up his post, a change-over which was delayed for some time due to problems on back-pay for the garrison, which Warwick finally resolved by paying the men himself from his own ample treasury. Rivers returned home, his Lieutenancy terminated, his estates in England's former Gallic Empire returned to French ownership, and his prospects more dependent than ever on his wife's liaison with Queen Margaret.

Sir Richard Woodville, 1st Earl Rivers.

(Detail from Garter Stall Plate)

CHAPTER THREE

"...Warwick rated him and said his father was but a squire
...and since then himself made by marriage..."

Paston Letters.

Jacquetta, now Baroness Rivers, had her eldest daughter's welfare to care for, as well as her husband's, and her happy association with Margaret of Anjou again paid dividends through the appointment of Elizabeth Woodville - still in her early teens - as a Maid of Honour to her Grace. The girl's future was further guaranteed when she agreed to marriage with Sir John Grey, heir to Edward Grey, Lord Ferrers of Groby. This happy event had taken place prior to her father's eviction from office in Calais and, by 1457 the first fruit of the marriage had appeared, a son who was named Thomas. Thus she was able to divide her time - quite happily, so tradition assures - between her duties as wife and mother at the Grey's Manor House of Bradgate and attendance on the Queen, most often at Margaret's favourite Palace at Greenwich.

However, war-clouds were again gathering over the Kingdom, where a feeble ruler was unable to contain, even if he had wished to do so, the unending extravagances of his young, headstrong wife - now mother to Edward, Prince of Wales, whose right to the succession, she felt, was threatened by Richard of York. Nor could Henry do anything to abate the enduring hatreds which lay between supporters of the two Plantagenet Houses and which, since First St Albans, had festered in a land where it had come to seem that might was right and justice only for the strong. A land, moreover, where French raiders could land and rob, rape, kill and burn almost, it appeared, at will.

King Henry and his Council, sensing that the country's descent into anarchy was becoming irreversible, brokered a Grand Reconciliation between the two sides, which took place at St Paul's on March 25th, 1458. Here the leaders of the two factions processed together, led by the King himself, York walking with the new Duke of Somerset, Salisbury with Wiltshire, and Warwick with the new Lord Clifford and all knelt, side by side, before the High Altar while Te Deum was sung for their new-found accord. The

**Jacquetta of Luxembourg, Duchess of Bedford,
1st Countess Rivers.**

(Artist's impression from medieval ms)

Jacquetta of Luxembourg's signature

formalities completed, the Yorkist leaders returned to their strongholds, York to his great Keep at Ludlow in the Welsh Marches, Salisbury to Middleham in North Yorkshire from where he could watch both the Border and Henry Percy of Northumberland, another whose father had died at St Albans fighting for the King. Warwick went to the key fortress in the ring, Calais, and the three waited and watched for the Queen's gambit.

Margaret's strategy was to continue to work through King and Council to weaken the enemy triumvirate as much as possible before striking. Warwick was summoned home in October, to answer charges of piracy, and narrowly avoided assassination at the meeting of Council called [apparently] to hear the evidence of his misdeeds. Salisbury found Percies and Westmorland Nevilles being appointed to positions of influence which had formerly been Middleham's perquisites, and in July, his younger brother, Robert Neville, Bishop of Durham had died and his appointed replacement to this very powerful position was Laurence Booth, a long-time servant of Queen Margaret. And, meantime, the Queen and her Lords were retaining knights, and enlisting men-at-arms and archers, until they were able to count on forces far outnumbering what strength York and his Neville allies could muster quickly, should the need ever arise.

In August, Richard Plantagenet, Duke of York sent urgent messages to Calais and Middleham calling on his kinsmen to join him at Ludlow as quickly as possible, if they wished to keep their estates, their wealth and, above all, their heads. The mighty war-machine planned by Margaret of Anjou was finally assembling to settle accounts with the Yorkist faction and, as its component parts moved towards their intended rendezvous in the Welsh border country, among them rode Sir John Grey, loyal supporter of Lancaster, and husband of Elizabeth Woodville.

Initially, events went well for the Yorkists. Salisbury leading a strong band of men-at-arms and archers to join his brother-in-law at Ludlow found his way blocked by Lords Audley and Dudley with a superior force, mainly Cheshire men, on a patch of open ground in Staffordshire, lying between Newcastle-under-Lyme and Market Drayton. The place was called Blore Heath and, on Sunday, September 23rd 1459 - St Matthews Day - it saw a mini-replica of Agincourt fought between two English generals who had both learned their soldiering trade in the French wars.

Emerging from a thickly wooded area, Salisbury saw the Lancastrian force arrayed for battle, blocking his path, and occupying higher ground. He quickly dismounted and deployed his own men into line of battle, their rear protected by the woods, the left flank by a ravine and the right by a laager of wagons, and awaited Audley's move. There was much shouting of defiance from both sides, and bellicose prancing and rearing of war-horses from the mainly mounted Lancastrian army, which led Salisbury to anticipate an imminent cavalry charge and he ordered his archers into the front rank to receive it, in place of his infantry. Audley, seeing the opposing men-at-arms apparently withdrawing towards the woods, ordered an immediate assault, leading his own division to attack the opposing left flank and sending orders to Dudley to cross the stream dividing the two armies with his division, and assail the enemy's right.

Charging down the slope before them, Audley's men reached the minor obstacle offered by the Wemberton Brook made much more hazardous by shelf after shelf of well-directed arrows from Salisbury's bowmen. And, as at Agincourt 44 years earlier, the front men went down, those behind crashed into them and fell, and total chaos resulted as flights of arrows continued to come whirring into the stricken ranks. Audley rallied his men for another effort, but they received the same treatment and broke when Audley was killed. By this time Dudley had got his division across the brook and after receiving the undivided attention of Salisbury's archers, tried to attack dismounted, but his much weakened force, discouraged and unsupported by the remnants of Audley's men - now intent on making the best of their way out of the fight - was soon in full flight away from the victorious Yorkists. The pursuit lasted for two hours and the eventual death toll numbered 2,000. Salisbury camped for the night on the field he had so signally won and two days later, without further interference, joined York at Ludlow. [*]

His son, the Earl of Warwick, had crossed from Calais and was marching quickly northwest through the midlands, to make his own junction with Salisbury and York. He had with him around 600 men from the Calais garrison under the immediate command of Andrew Trollope, an experienced campaigner with initiative and a well-developed sense of self-preservation, as would be made evident in the near future. The Calais men were fortunate not to have an early meeting with a much stronger contingent of the King's army, led by the Duke of Somerset, the two parties passing each other unwittingly near Coleshill and continuing to their respective destinations.

[*] For more detailed accounts of Blore Heath, see "The Hollow Crowns" and "The Lordly Ones" by the same Author.]

After they reached Ludlow, however, Trollope was contacted by secret letter from Somerset, in which the Duke pointed out that Warwick's clear purpose was to join with his relatives in attacking the King, rather than helping to defend family property, and that such treasonable activity was punishable by death. He suggested that the prudent course would be for Trollope, and as many of his men as wished to accompany him, to take advantage of the Duke's offer to intercede with King Henry on their behalf, if they would "return to their proper allegiance". Shortly afterwards, the Yorkist army moved out of Ludlow Castle, where there was insufficient room to house and supply such a force, and constructed a defensible position some miles to the south at Ludford Bridge, there to await the expected onset of the King's men. Somerset's much larger army arrived at dusk and drew up in battle order, facing the Yorkist's position. During the night, Trollope and his 600 men-at-arms slipped quietly out of the earthworks and moved over to the other side, where they were welcomed heartily by Somerset. Their defection was discovered before first-light by the Yorkist leaders, who found the rest of their army already following the melting process started by Trollope, and realised their only safety lay in immediate flight.

Leaving his wife and younger children in Ludlow, feeling that they would be reasonably safe in the magnanimous hands of King Henry, Richard of York took his second son, Edmund, Earl of Rutland, and made for the west coast and thence on to Dublin, where he had secure refuge. Salisbury and Warwick, with York's eldest son, Edward, Earl of March, made for the southwest and from there, accompanied by one of Warwick's leading sea-captains, John Dynham, took sailing boat to Calais, which haven - held firmly for York by William Neville, Warwick's uncle - they reached without further incident.

Their objective secured by the simple threat of overwhelming force, the Lancastrian Lords returned to their estates with the sense of a job well done. York, Warwick and Salisbury were attainted as traitors in a November Parliament called at Coventry and their goods and estates declared forfeit to the Crown. Cecily Neville and her younger children were committed to the custody of her sister Anne, Duchess of Buckingham, and there was a great sharing-out of the offices formerly held by the Yorkist leaders and their adherents. As part of this process, Henry Beaufort, Duke of Somerset, was named to the key post of Captain of Calais and lost no time in assembling a small fleet and setting sail for France to assume his new, important dignity.

Unfortunately, he arrived some days after the three Earls and was accorded a hot, rather than warm, welcome.

Beaufort moved along the coast to Guisnes, taking Trollope and his men from the garrison, who formed the main strength of his force, with him and sent to England for reinforcement. Again unfortunate, his anchored fleet was overtaken by a sudden Channel storm and swept back along the coast, ending in the doubtful sanctuary of Calais harbour. Helpless under Warwick's artillery, the sailors surrendered and Somerset and his men were effectively marooned in Guisnes until a new fleet could be assembled and sent to their relief. This process took some two months and, about Christmas, Warwick learned that a relieving-force had been put together and was waiting on the weather in Sandwich harbour. It was commanded by Richard Woodville, Lord Rivers, erstwhile Lieutenant of Calais, who had with him his son, Sir Anthony Woodville, now nearing 20 years of age and eager to widen his experience and make his mark in great affairs. This he would shortly do, though not in a way he would have anticipated, much less chosen.

During his period of Office as Captain of Calais, the Earl of Warwick had recruited a number of very experienced sea-captains to command the fleet he maintained in the port so making it indeed a dagger aimed at the England's heart through the control of the shortest passage between it and the Continent. Two of these commanders, John Dynham and John Wenlock, were now sent to raid Sandwich and to destroy the relief force so labouriously assembled there. This the pair did brilliantly in an early-morning raid on January 15th, 1460, where they succeeded in capturing or sinking all the fleet and bringing their prizes back to the haven of Calais. Along with this precious booty, they brought Lord Rivers and his son as captives, the pair having been captured aboard their flagship.

The Earls were delighted by this success and quickly assembled the townsfolk and the garrison in the town square to see the living tokens of their victory and to witness their further humiliation. Writing of this event later, William Paston said "...my lord Rivers was brought to Calais and before the lords with eight score torches, and there my Lord of Salisbury rated him, calling him knave's son, that he should be so rude to call him and these other lords traitors, for they shall be found the king's true liegemen when he should be found a traitor. And my Lord of Warwick rated him and said that his father was but a squire and brought up with King Henry the Fifth, and sithen himself made by marriage, and also made lord, and that it was not his part to have such language of lords, being of the king's blood. And my Lord of March rated him in like wise. And Sir Anthony [Woodville] was rated for his language of all three lords in like wise..." All of which contumely was perfectly true, though Rivers may have detected some irony in being rated as one "made by marriage" by a man who was, undoubtedly, in exactly the same case. However, if he did, he was wise enough not to say so.

Nevertheless, both Woodvilles were sent to durance-vile in the fortress of Calais, where they no doubt spent a thoroughly miserable time. But, they came to no further physical harm, since they had been commissioned in their duties by King Henry VI to whom Salisbury, Warwick and March were "true liegemen". They were held prisoner in Calais for six months, during which time Warwick's captains held the Channel for York and their command of the sea permitted the Earl to visit his uncle, Richard of York, in his Dublin sanctuary and to synchronise plans for the return of the four leaders to England. The first phase of their design was carried out on June 27th, when the three Earls, accompanied this time by Lord Fauconberg and 2,000 men-at-arms and archers, crossed from Calais to Sandwich and landed proclaiming their continuing loyalty to King Henry and that they came only "for their own". With them in their train came the hapless Lord Rivers and Anthony Woodville, who were shortly released to be reunited with their loving family. The Earls had more important affairs to attend to than putting further humiliation on vulgar upstarts who dared to meddle in the affairs of those with the blood-royal in their veins. Their time would come, but, for now, the urgent need was to face the Lancastrian enemy again and, this time, to emerge victorious.

Coat of Arms of
Sir Anthony Woodville

**Richard Neville, Earl of Warwick, the Kingmaker, as a "Weeper" figure
on the tomb of his father-in-law Richard Beauchamp**

(Geoffrey Wheeler)

CHAPTER FOUR

"...My title's good, and better far than his.."
[Henry VI pt 3]

Within a week of their landing, the Yorkists had marched through Kent, gathering eager recruits along the way, and made a triumphant entry into London. The King, with his wife and son, was in Coventry and his main supporters were scattered, tending to their own estates, the return of the dispossessed Earls had been well timed. However, Warwick, now emerging as the master-planner of his faction, knew that Queen Margaret would not be long in rousing the King to action and, by July 3rd, leaving Salisbury with a strong force to watch Lord Scales, who held the Tower for the King, he and the young giant Edward of March moved north, with Fauconberg and an advance guard probing before them.

King Henry had indeed been spurred to swift action by his wife and, having gathered a force judged sufficient to deal with anything the rebel Earls might have with them, had marched from Coventry and, by July 8th, had reached Northampton. The march had been hard for England was suffering under one of its wettest Summers for many a long day and the roads were often quagmire rather than highway. In addition, Henry's army had with it a number of great guns, which, it was hoped would overawe and outmatch anything the Yorkists might be able to put into the field, but which were proving a sore burden in the soft conditions underfoot. The King and his main commander, Humphrey Stafford, Duke of Buckingham decided, therefore, to encamp and rest their troops and crossed to the south bank of the River Nene, where they constructed a horse-shoe earthwork, embrasured to take their cannons and here they would wait the arrival of the oncoming Yorkists.

While Buckingham and King Henry were supervising the construction of their fortified encampment, Warwick and Edward had reached Towcester, where Fauconberg rejoined them and reported the proximity of the royal army. The Earls moved forward to Hunsbury Hill and made night-camp there, anticipating battle on the following day, July 10th, 1460. Nonetheless, in the morning, Warwick sent embassies to the King; the first, led by the Bishop of

Salisbury returned unsuccessful, so he sent a second led by the Archbishop of Canterbury, accompanied by a Papal Legate. The Archbishop's efforts to bring about a peaceful outcome proved entirely abortive, ending in a sharp exchange of words with Buckingham, who threatened that if the Earl of Warwick approached the King he would pay for his temerity with his life, to which Warwick sent response that he would speak with his King at two of the clock or die in the attempt, and both sides armed for battle. King Henry's position looked forbidding in the extreme, its rear protected by the flooded river and its front by trenches and sharpened wooden stakes. And, at regular intervals along the face of the works were the great guns carried there with such labour from Coventry. Less happily for the King, the incessant rain had left the cannon-embrasures water-logged, a fact which had been noted by the Yorkist commanders who felt - rightly as it transpired - that the guns would not be able to fire on their attacking line. Promptly at 2.00 p.m., therefore, the rebel army marched forward to the attack. They would speak with the King - or die. Unusually, the attackers had arrayed their force in two divisions, one behind the other, which went forward on a narrow front with the young Edward leading the van and Warwick with the troops in reserve. Immediately, Edward attacked the King's left front where Buckingham commanded, but was so hampered by the slippery ground and furious fire from the opposing archers that he fell back and tried again on the other flank. Here, the commander was Grey of Ruthyn and, with less interference from the archers, Edward's men quickly reached the earthworks. Then, almost as if it were pre-arranged, their opponents followed the example of Trollope's men at Ludford Bridge, pulling down the barricades to admit the Yorkists and then joining with them in attacking Buckingham's division. The fighting was soon over. Many of the King's army were killed in the following rout and still more drowned in the flooding Nene, which from protecting back-plate had suddenly become an entrapment for the beaten army. Among the dead lay the bodies of Humphrey Stafford, first Duke of Buckingham and uncle by marriage to Edward and to Warwick, the Earl of Shrewsbury, Lord Egremont, brother to the Earl of Northumberland, and John, Viscount Beaumont. King Henry had survived unscathed and meekly received the homage of his conquerors, who took him with them back to London, for his greater protection.

In the next four months, Warwick took firm hold of the reins of government - at least, in London and the south. In the north, however, his writ was ignored and Clifford and Northumberland gathered men and bided their time. So too in the west where Somerset and the Earl of Devon were recruiting and Queen Margaret, from her refuge with Jasper Tudor, Earl of Pembroke, was setting Wales alight and pulling all the strands together by letters constantly couriered to south and north. As the Winter evenings shortened, Margaret, stunned by news from London, moved to Yorkshire and summoned all supporters of Lancaster to join her there.

Warwick, sensing the ever-growing need for parliamentary action to reinforce his party's governance, had summoned the Estates to meet in London on October 7th and sent urgently to Richard, Duke of York, still waiting in Dublin, that the time had come for him to return and lead his faction. Three days after the Parliament had opened, York made a royal entrance into London and passed through cheering crowds to the Palace of Westminster, where, to Warwick's astonishment - and fury - he made public his claim to the crown of England. For days, arguments over the rights and wrongs of York's case were debated and the stalemate was finally broken by an Act of Accord in which York agreed that Henry should continue to rule during his life-time but that, on his death, the House of York would retake their rightful place on England's throne.

The Act, meekly signed by Henry in his unending quest for peace, eliminated his own son's right to succeed him, a resignation of kingly power which his wife could not accept and she rode north determined to reinstate her young son Edward's right to rule in his father's place. And, if this meant that Warwick must die and that York and all his brood must die, then so be it. Margaret of Anjou would do whatever she must to maintain the power of Lancaster over English land.

Through December, the growing Lancastrian army - northerners, Scots, Welsh, westcountrymen - lived off the land in Yorkshire, mainly off the estates of Richard of York and his brother-in- law, Richard Neville, Earl of Salisbury. The two Lords, angry at the damage to their property and people and not appreciating the strength of Margaret's forces, left London with 3,000 men and reached Sandal Castle, near Wakefield, in time to spend Christmas within its walls. On December 29th, Margaret, encamped at Pontefract, 12 miles to the east of Sandal, heard of York's arrival and moved with as many of her men as could be mustered quickly, appearing before Sandal in the late afternoon of the day following.

The Yorkist leaders had sent parties out foraging and scouting and their return was imminent; the supplies and intelligence they would provide must fall into Lancastrian hands unless immediate, remedial action were taken, and York and Salisbury, with their sons, the Earl of Rutland and Sir Thomas Neville, armed, arrayed their men and charged down the hill into the heart of the host of Lancaster. Briefly successful, the onslaught slowed, halted and was buried by the enemy's superior numbers. All thoughts turned to escape, but it was too late and the would-be King Richard died, along with his son and nephew and most of his men. Salisbury was taken for ransom and sent to Pontefract, where his life ended the following morning at the hands of a lynch-mob. Margaret and her great army, having restored much of Lancaster's pride in one brief hour, turned south for London, where Warwick waited.

It took six weeks for the army of Lancaster to reach St Albans, gateway to London, and there they were met by Richard Neville, Earl of Warwick, and now of Salisbury, with a strong, but smaller army, which Warwick had divided into four divisions spread over a two-mile front and, in the end, all facing in the wrong direction. Through chance and a night-march, Margaret's superior force took the Yorkist army entirely by surprise, and in the rear, and rolled-up the four divisions in detail. With a remnant, Warwick escaped eastwards to join with Edward of March, who had won a famous victory at Mortimer's Cross and was marching to add his men to Warwick's.

The two made quickly for London, which they reached before the Lancastrians, much to the relief of the citizens who knew of the 30-mile-wide swathe Margaret's army had cut through 150 miles of England on their march south. Thwarted of their promised loot and unable to take London without siege equipment, the army of Lancaster, taking King Henry - who had sat happily under a tree while Second St Albans raged around him - back with them, headed north for the friendlier territory in Yorkshire. With them rode Sir John Grey, husband of Elizabeth Woodville, moving towards his own, last, fateful performance in the unfolding drama of York and Lancaster.

CHAPTER FIVE

"...One way or other, she is for a king;
and she shall be my love, or else my queen..."
[Henry VI Pt 3]

In the aftermath of Towton, the leaders of the Lancastrian army and faction - dead or fled - were attainted of treason, making their goods and estates subject to confiscation by the Crown, much to the profit of the new King and his supporters. Among those adjudged guilty of treason, through the bearing of arms against Edward IV, was the late Sir John Grey, Baron Ferrers of Groby, and his estate, including the fair manor of Bradgate, was forfeit to the royal Treasury. Lady Elizabeth Grey, his widow, rendered penniless thereby, had little alternative but to return, with her two sons, Thomas and Richard, to her family's home at Grafton.

And, even here, there was little apparent security, since Elizabeth's father, Lord Rivers, and her oldest brother, Sir Anthony Woodville, were also caught in the general purging of Lancastrians and were attainted and their possessions escheated under a patent issued on May 14th, little more than six weeks after the defeat at Towton. For the Woodville family - but lately arrived in the corridors of power - it seemed that the best they could contemplate for the future was a return to life as country squires, holders of minor Offices under Crown or County, comparative nobodies. A sad pass for such an ambitious brood to come to.

However, they had yet one remaining asset : the persuasive skills, the joyous femininity, and the unfading beauty of the matriarch of the family, Baroness Rivers, Jacquetta of Luxembourg. The female wiles which had worked on the courtiers of the young King Henry, to the benefit of her clandestine husband and the first child of her most fruitful marriage, might still be brought into play with the impressionable young King Edward. And, during a brief recreational excursion to Stony Stratford - a short ride from Grafton Regis - in June, the King wrote to his Chancellor, telling him that he had pardoned Lord Rivers, and the official confirmation of this charity was subsequently dated July 12th, 1461. Further, the King wrote to his Treasurer "affectionately considering the state and benefit of Jacquetta Duchess of

Bedford and Lord Rivers, of his especial grace", instructing him to reinstate the annual stipend of over 300 marks paid to the Duchess, as the widow of a royal Prince, and stipulating that 100 pounds of this should be made immediately available.

The Woodvilles who only a year previously, in Calais, had been "rated" by the then Earl of March as parvenu nobodies, who, but three months earlier, were ruined as attainted traitors, were once again installed as persons of some consequence and substance, and in the favour of their new King. A King who would scarcely have missed noting, during his visit, the attraction of the family's eldest daughter with her serene but sorrowful presence and her little boys round her. He would certainly find occasion to call at Grafton Manor again.

Thus it was that Elizabeth Grey did not follow the normal course of the time for a widowed lady - particularly one with claims to beauty and evidence of fertility. In brief, there was no immediate re-marriage. Perhaps this was due to problems with her dower, which was tied up in litigation with tenants of the property which had been deeded to her late husband by her father-in-law for their upkeep; a process lengthened later by further suit brought by her former mother-in-law and her second husband Sir John Bourchier. Perhaps it resulted from a rumoured secret liaison with one, Jocelyn Hardwicke, a distant cousin of her husband, of which nothing of any real substance ever came to light.

Perhaps it was something else entirely.

After the year of rebellion and royal reaction, marching and counter-marching, pillage and rapine, battle and sudden death which followed the return of Warwick and Edward from Calais, England became a quieter, pleasanter, safer place to live. Even the weather, which could scarcely have been worse, improved. There was still some minor bickering in the Welsh Marches, speedily dealt with by Sir William Herbert, and more serious actions from time to time, along the Border with Scotland, where Lancastrian fugitives allied with Scots and French mercenaries made regular attacks on the estates, towns and castles of northern England. Here the Nevilles of Middleham held the line for York with Richard, Earl of Warwick, at his best in his favourite role of arch-schemer and strategic-thinker, and his younger brother, John, Lord Montagu, as the vastly experienced, hard-fighting general in the field.

Through much of 1462, the Neville brothers, aided by their uncle William, now Earl of Kent, and the King's close friend, Lord William Hastings, had counter-raided into Scotland and laid siege to all the castles south of the Border which were held for Lancaster. By Christmas-tide, all but Alnwick had surrendered and even the great stronghold of the Percies fell in the first month of 1463. Henry Beaufort, Duke of Somerset, was among those captured and, sent to the King for judgement, had exercised his Plantagenet charm on Edward and become a boon companion. Warwick felt able to go south again to immerse himself in the work he loved best, the governance of England and the constant diplomatic manoeuvring, the simultaneous chess-games with France and Burgundy.

As May ended, Warwick had to ride quickly for the north as news came that a strong force of Scots, French and Lancastrians had crossed the Border and three main fortresses had surrendered to their army as soon as they were summoned. Again, the combined generalship of the two Nevilles sufficed to give their opponents a severe trouncing and Montagu pursued them many miles into Scotland in a punitive raid which soon had the Scots' King suing for a renewed truce. King Edward came north to sign the new treaty on December 9th and heard from his cousins that Margaret of Anjou, finally despairing of her cause in Scotland had fled to France, taking her son with her. King Henry was besieged in Bamburgh Castle, the north was again secure and, once more, the Earl of Warwick departed for London, just as the Spring buds of 1464 burst into blossom.

And, once more, the embers of Lancastrian revolt burst into flame, this time fanned by Henry Beaufort who had reverted to his old allegiance and joining King Henry in Bamburgh, was constantly raiding the surrounding countryside and gathering recruits from both sides of the Border. Montagu sent word to the King and his brother of what had developed and assured them that he had sufficient force to contain whatever trouble Beaufort and the rest of the Lancastrian rump could make. There was currently no need for either to hasten northwards to his support, which was fortunate, for King Edward had more pleasant diversions in view for the first day of May. On his leisurely way north to join with Montagu and Warwick, he halted at Stony Stratford and thence to Grafton Regis, where Edward Plantagenet took to wife Elizabeth Grey, nee Woodville.

The ceremony was short and simple. In addition to the couple and the priest, Thomas Leson, the local incumbent, were present: Jacquetta of

Luxembourg, two gentlemen, "and a young man who helped the priest to sing". Afterwards, Edward returned almost immediately to Stony Stratford from where, two days later, he wrote to Lord Rivers saying he proposed to lodge at Grafton for a short time, and was received with all honour on his arrival later that day. The next four days were spent in hunting and feasting, and the bridal pair met secretly each night, Elizabeth being conducted to the King's bedchamber by her mother, Jacquetta.

Edward then moved on to Leicester where he spent a week waiting for levies to rendezvous with the rest of his force and set out for the north on May 15th. Coincidentally, this was the same day that Montagu brought lasting peace to the Border country, when he comprehensively defeated the Lancastrian army at a field appropriately called the Levels a few miles to the southeast of the small market town of Hexham. In a postscript to his report, he told the King that the double-traitor Beaufort would no longer present a problem, since he had paid the ultimate price for his treachery in Hexham market square, immediately after the battle.

The King was vastly pleased with Montagu's news and, on arrival in York, he created the victorious John Neville Earl of Northumberland and with the title, gave him all the estates and castles previously pertaining to the Percy family. He then went with Richard and John Neville to Middleham where he spent a few pleasurable days, riding, hunting and feasting with his kinfolk, before setting out again for the south and stopping shortly en route to take Skipton Castle, which, like Henry Beaufort, had returned briefly to its Lancastrian roots.

And, in all the time he was with them, Edward said not a word to either of the Neville Lords about his diversion to Grafton Regis. They would have to know about it in due time, but Edward disliked family quarrels and he knew his coupling with the Lancastrian Woodvilles, through the daughter of the man Warwick had scorned at Calais, must provide considerable cause for friction when it became known. However, the die was cast and he would cross the bridges as he came to them. Meantime, he proceeded on his way south to London, with a pleasant dalliance in Grafton Regis, en route, in the forefront of his mind.

CHAPTER SIX

"... to know his meaning, they asked him, smiling, with whom
he wished to ally himself, and he replied...the daughter
of Lord Rivers..."

[Receuil des Chroniques, Waurin]

Before the Summer was out, the north was pacified and Warwick, having dealt with domestic affairs at Middleham and in Warwickshire, moved to London with the intention of further developing his own master-plan for the rule of the Kingdom. It was time the King took a wife and this view the great Earl raised at a meeting of the Council on September 4th. His fellow councillors agreed with him and with his preference for an alliance with France through marriage with Bona of Savoy, sister-in-law of Louis XI. This connection had been a favourite project of Warwick for some time past and he had actively promoted it during visits to the French court, and in discussions with visiting embassies from Louis. He had already completed plans to visit Paris again in the following month and urged upon Edward the necessity for a decision so that he could finalise arrangements which were already well-advanced.

The King responded that he agreed it was time for him to wed, but he wondered whether his councillors would approve his choice of bride. When they pressed him for details, he - laughing - said he would take to wife the daughter of Lord Rivers, Lady Elizabeth Grey. This announcement drew consternation from all corners of the chamber and comments and exchanges grew progressively heated until, to quell the growing swell of criticism, Edward told them that he was talking of a fait accompli, the Lancastrian widow was already his wife and, thereby, effective Queen of England.

The grand designs of the Earl of Warwick and much of his prestige and status in the eyes of Lords and rulers at home and overseas had been diminished at a stroke by this big, handsome, laughing hero, who owed his very throne to the efforts of, and risks taken by, Richard Neville - at least, that was the view of the Earl of Warwick and Salisbury. However, Warwick was ever a realist and when Edward, three weeks after the Council meeting,

Elizabeth Woodville, Queen of England.

(Detail from the Royal Window, Canterbury Cathedral)

formally presented the new Queen to his court, she was led in solemn procession into the chapel of Westminster Abbey with George, Duke of Clarence, and Richard Neville, Earl of Warwick, holding her by the hand, and there, all present acknowledged her as Queen.

Grateful for Warwick's apparent easy acceptance of his escapade, Edward made efforts to ensure the continuing regard of his powerful cousin and George Neville, brother to the Earl and already Edward's Chancellor, was translated from the See of Exeter to the vacant Archbishopric of York. Nonetheless, the new Queen's influence with Edward quickly became apparent through the arrangement of favourable marriages for her sisters and brothers to the wealthy and powerful among England's aristocracy. It was clear that soon, the family of Jacquetta, Lady Rivers, would be as well-connected and influential in England as were her siblings in France. And, over the next two years, it became ever-clearer to the Earl of Warwick that Woodvilles' gains were largely to Nevilles' cost.

Immediately after Edward had made his marriage known and formally presented his wife to the court, plans were put in hand for her coronation which was eventually set for the Sunday before Whitsun, May 26th, 1465, and would be celebrated in Westminster Abbey. It was important to the King and his new Queen that the ceremonial pertaining to this great occasion should be as magnificent and awe-inspiring as human ingenuity could make it and no effort or expense was spared to this end. In particular, it was essential to stress Elizabeth's noble - even royal - antecedents and since this could not be achieved through her father's side, all emphasis would be laid on her maternal line through Jacquetta of Luxembourg, Duchess of Bedford.

Jacquetta was the eldest daughter of Pierre of Luxembourg, who, as Count of St Pol had been among the most important of England's allies during the Hundred Years War and a close friend of Henry V. Her uncle, Jean, was one of the leading military commanders of the day and had led the force which captured Joan of Arc at Compiegne, imprisoned her and eventually handed her over - some say "sold" her - to the English, who, in turn, passed her, and decisions on her fate, to the pastoral care of the Burgundian Church. Another uncle, Louis, Bishop of Therouanne, was involved in Joan's trial and was "moved to tears" by her testimony there, but did nothing to deliver her from her cruel fate. He did however, play a key role in arranging Jacquetta's marriage to John, Duke of Bedford, which ceremony was held in Louis' own Cathedral.

To stress Queen Elizabeth's descent from such distinguished forebears, Philip, Duke of Burgundy, was asked to send a suitable delegation to the ceremony, preferably led by her uncle, Jacquetta's youngest brother, Jacques de Luxembourg, Lord of Richeburg. The Duke was happy to comply with Edward's personal request and Queen Elizabeth's familial background was duly embellished by the presence of her uncle Jacques and the imposing train of a hundred fellow nobles and equerries, which he brought with him to Westminster.

The ceremony was also graced by members of the noble houses supporting the Yorkist cause, some Nevilles, the Dukes of Norfolk and Suffolk, Bourchier, Earl of Essex, and FitzAlan, Earl of Arundel, with his heir, Thomas, Lord Maltravers. Families long-faithful to Lancaster were also represented through Henry Stafford, the boy-Duke of Buckingham, and the young Earl of Oxford, John de Vere, carrying out his traditional, special duties as Great Chamberlain and Queen's Chamberlain. And, still beautiful, vivacious, sparkling with life, despite nearing 50 years of age, Jacquetta of Luxembourg shed her own special brilliance over the occasion.

Elizabeth Woodville's instatement as Queen of England was a magnificent spectacle carried out with all due solemnity and regard for tradition and celebrated by feasting, pageants, singing of choirs and piping of minstrels, and scattering of largesse among participants and spectators alike. Richard Neville, Earl of Warwick, did not attend, being unavoidably absent on a diplomatic mission for his royal master to Burgundy and France and the Earl's overt dislike for the Queen would find much to feed upon during the coming two years. Margaret Woodville, the Queen's sister, had married in the October of the previous year Thomas Maltravers, heir to the Earldom of Arundel; likewise her brother, John, had married the Dowager Duchess of Norfolk - nearly three times his age - in January 1465 and incidentally, thereby became uncle to both Warwick and to his brother-in-law, Edward IV. In 1466, Katherine Woodville in her mid-teens married the still-younger Henry Stafford, Duke of Buckingham, and Mary married William Herbert, heir to Lord Herbert, newly created Earl of Pembroke, while a year later, Anne Woodville married William Bourchier, heir to the Essex Earldom.

For more than two centuries past, the Nevilles had increased their wealth and power through marriages, judiciously arranged, and this policy had appeared to reach its apogee in the alliances of Ralph, first Earl of Westmorland, with Joan Beaufort, only daughter of John of Gaunt, of his son, Richard Neville the elder, with the heiress of Salisbury, and of his grandson Richard with the eventual heiress of Warwick. Now, their position in the realm was being usurped by a family of nobodies, who had captured the King Warwick had made, and were eagerly following the same path to power which the Nevilles themselves had pioneered.

The Earl of Warwick returned from his continental tour at the beginning of July, having agreed an 18 month truce with Louis of France but not having succeeded in persuading Burgundy to renounce further support for the Lancastrian cause. Edward and his Queen were on pilgrimage to Canterbury at the time and here they received news of the capture of Henry VI, who had been a fugitive since Hexham and had been found hiding in Lancashire. The former King was brought speedily to London, where Warwick met the escorting train at Islington and personally conducted Henry to his place of confinement in the Tower. The son of Henry V re-entered his capital with no ceremony; he was travel-stained, dirty, and with his legs tied to the stirrups of his mount cut a pathetic figure indeed, as the great, splendidly-attired Earl of Warwick led him through gaping crowds to a captivity which was to endure for most of the seven years of life, which, ironically, were all that was left to both of them

On February 11th of the following year, the first fruit of the royal union appeared, a princess. At Edward's invitation, Warwick stood as her godfather, while his brother George, Archbishop of York, christened her after her mother, Elizabeth, portents perhaps of reconciliation between the King and his most powerful supporters. However, within a month, Warwick's nominee and uncle by marriage, Lord Mountjoy, was replaced as Treasurer by Lord Rivers, the former Richard Woodville, whom Warwick and Edward had soundly and publicly berated in Calais market-place as a jumped-up popinjay. Shortly afterwards, perhaps in further recompense for these preceding insults, Edward was pleased to create his father-in-law, Earl Rivers.

And then came the unkindest cut of all. The son of Warwick's brother John, Lord Montagu and newly-made Earl of Northumberland, the victor of

Hexham, young George Neville, had been contracted to marry Anne Holland, heiress to the rich Dukedom of Exeter, a union typical of Neville family policy and conceived by Warwick himself. Unhappily, this long-standing arrangement was cancelled by Anne's mother on receiving a payment of 4,000 marks from Elizabeth Woodville, whose elder son, Thomas Grey, replaced the young Neville as bridegroom to be and the wedding took place on October 1st, 1466.

Clearly, the time had come for Warwick to take any and all steps necessary to the restoration of his and his family's pre-eminence in England and it would go hard with any of the Woodville clan who crossed him in his rightful purpose.

Royal Seal of Elizabeth Woodville.

(Geoffrey Wheeler)

CHAPTER SEVEN

"Alas poor Clarence ! Is it for a wife that thou art malcontent?
I will provide thee."

[Henry VI, pt 3]

The Earl of Warwick, having lost his over-riding influence on Edward the King to the Queen and her family, turned his thoughts to the two younger Princes of the House of York. George, Duke of Clarence, and Richard, Duke of Gloucester, would soon be of an age to marry and they were ideally suited in every way to be matched with his own daughters, Isabel and Anne. If these unions could be arranged then it should not be beyond the wit and powers of the greatest peer in the realm to unmake the King he had made amid the ruin of Second St Albans and replace him with his younger brother, George of Clarence. Warwick felt he would have little difficulty "guiding" the pleasure-loving Duke in the way he should go, particularly when his private ear was controlled by the Earl's own daughter.

Towards the Christmas-time of 1466 therefore, Warwick invited the two young men to visit him and his family at Cambridge, and to take an extended holiday with them, during which the two young couples, who had known each other since childhood, were often thrown together in merry dalliance. News of this soon reached the King's ear and he sent word to George and Richard that they should return to London without more delay. When his brothers arrived, Edward questioned them closely on events during their visit to Cambridge and asked them whether there had been any discussion of marriage. Both denied that there had been such talk, but the King made clear that he did not believe this and, speaking as their monarch as well as head of their family, he told them that there could be no marriages with the daughters of Richard Neville.

Richard, ever-eager to please his hero-brother, agreed without demur, but George, now past his 18th birthday, was less passive, pointing out that Isabel was an excellent match for him, the wealthiest heiress in England and, to boot, a very pretty girl who would soon be 16, amply old enough to wed. However, Edward would hear no more and firmly forbade his brothers to have further contact with their Neville cousins. George accepted with ill grace, but he continued to keep in touch with the Earl of Warwick, with whom he clearly had much in common. Edward did not like this, but there was not much to be done about it immediately and he had need again of Warwick's diplomatic skills and contacts to discuss renegotiation of the truce with France, which was drawing to its end. This would serve a dual purpose, separating Warwick and Clarence for the time being and getting Richard Neville out of England while the King pursued a very different line of foreign policy in secret discussions with Burgundy.

The establishment of closer relations with her natal land was a matter close to the heart of Jacquetta of Luxembourg, Duchess of Bedford and, therefore, to her extended family in England. Edward IV had a warm regard for his mother-in-law and through direct discussion with him and the additional influence she could bring to bear through her daughter Elizabeth, Jacquetta was able to bias him in favour of an alliance with Burgundy. Fortunately for her, such a course also sat well with the people of England since the prosperity of their trade in wool and woollen cloth depended largely on the Burgundian connection. Thus it was that, when the Earl of Warwick sailed for France to carry out the mission given to him by his King, in furtherance of a policy which Warwick himself had advanced, a large deputation from the Burgundian court arrived in London, apparently for no greater purpose than chivalrous contention between Anthony, Lord Scales, the Queen's brother, and the Bastard of Burgundy. Included in the Bastard's party was, naturally, Jacques of Luxembourg, brother of the Duchess of Bedford.

After the jousting at the Smithfield Tournament, feasting and merriment were the order of the day and Edward and his Queen hosted a grand supper in the Grocers' Hall on June 12th to which 80 beauteous young noblewomen were invited, "the least of them being daughter of a Baron...and Monsieur the Bastard and his people feasted greatly and honourably". A reciprocal dinner hosted by the Bastard was planned for the following Sunday, with the presence of the Queen and her sisters being particularly requested, but this entertainment was abruptly cancelled when news arrived of the death of Philip, Duke of Burgundy on the 15th of the month. The Bastard and his party left England for home on June 21st and though their departure was overshadowed by the demise of the ruler of Burgundy, they left with their mission well accomplished.

The Earl of Warwick arrived back in England at the beginning of July, bringing with him an embassy from Louis XI of France which expected to work out the detail of the treaty of peace Warwick had negotiated at Edward's request. To his chagrin, he found that all his efforts had been set at naught. During his absence, his brother George had been replaced as Chancellor, negotiations for a treaty with Burgundy were rapidly nearing completion and this alliance would be reinforced within a year through the marriage of Margaret, Edward's sister, to Charles the Bold, the new Duke of Burgundy.

Louis' ambassadors were largely ignored by the court, though they were granted a short excursion to Windsor on August 12th to witness the baptism of a second daughter born to Elizabeth Woodville. The new Princess was named Mary and two days after attending her christening, the French nobles returned to their master after having enjoyed some six weeks of lavish entertainment provided for them entirely by the Earl of Warwick and George of Clarence, but otherwise empty-handed. Richard Neville moved north to the heartland of his strength in the north of Yorkshire and in his great fortress at Middleham he thought and schemed and planned towards the day when he should have his revenge on Woodvilles and King alike. They should all be made to see who was the real master in England.

Warwick's absence from court made easier the negotiations with Burgundy on the terms of the marriage planned between Margaret of York and Duke Charles. Anthony Woodville, Elizabeth's oldest brother, Lord Scales in right of his wife, was sent with a mission to Burgundy in late September to finalise details with Duke Charles and, on October 1st, the Princess Margaret attended a meeting of the Grand Council to give her formal consent to the marriage. Jacquetta's plans for ever-closer links between England and Burgundy were prospering indeed.

Meantime, the Earl of Warwick was busying himself, amongst other matters, with marriage plans of his own. George of Clarence had found time to visit Middleham for talks with Warwick and, as a result, application was made to Pope Pius II for dispensation of the prohibition on marriages within specified degrees of consanguinity in respect of a proposed union between George of Clarence and his cousin once removed, Isabel Neville. Word of this reached Edward and he lodged formal opposition in Rome to the granting of such exemption. Further, as the Christmas festivities came round once more and another new year dawned, Edward sent to Warwick summoning the Earl to join him at court. Warwick would have none of this and replied that he would never again come to the Council while his enemies sat therein, and named specifically Richard Woodville, Earl Rivers, Anthony Woodville, Lord Scales and Sir John Woodville, husband to the Dowager of Norfolk, together with Lord Herbert as his deadly adversaries.

Fruits of Warwick's planning in other fields also began to emerge during January 1468. Henry Courtenay, heir to the Earl of Devon who had fallen at Towton, joined with Thomas Hungerford whose father died at Hexham, in raising the standard of Lancaster in the west country. Their revolt was quickly put down by Lord Stafford, who was given the Devon title in reward. Jasper Tudor, half-brother to Henry VI and Earl of Pembroke likewise raised the Welsh Dragon Banner and, with French help, took Harlech Castle and sacked Denbigh. This revolt was equally quickly dealt with by Lord Herbert, who was rewarded with the attainted Tudor's title of Earl of Pembroke. But the times were clearly unsettled and Edward, sensing the master-hand of Warwick behind the problems that were besetting his Kingdom, tried again to be reconciled with the Earl.

This time, the King asked George Neville, Archbishop of York, to mediate with his brother and, following increasingly friendly contacts through this channel, Richard Neville again appeared at court and in Council and, when Margaret of York set out on June 18th to journey to Burgundy for her marriage, she rode the first stage sitting pillion behind the Earl of Warwick. After spending a few days at the monastery at Stratford Langthorne, the Duchess of Burgundy-to-be embarked at Margate on the *New Ellen* for passage to Sluys. Neither Warwick nor any of the Nevilles accompanied Margaret overseas; instead Anthony, Lord Scales, would formally present her at the Burgundian court, assisted by his brother John Woodville. The marriage took place on July 3rd - exactly one year after Warwick's return from his fruitless mission to France - and the following celebrations lasted for nine days. Amidst the usual chivalrous breaking of lances, John Woodville maintained the family's reputation for expertise in such knightly pursuits by carrying off the chief prize.

While the younger Woodvilles were thus enjoying themselves in their mother's native land, the rest of the family had important affairs to transact in

London. Earlier that month, a man named Cornelius, servant to Sir Robert Whitingham, who was with Margaret of Anjou's court-in-exile, was caught carrying letters from the Lancastrians to friends in the Capital. He was sent to the Tower for questioning and, under torture, identified a number of prominent Londoners as sympathetic to Lancaster. In his list, he included the name of John Hawkins, a servant of Lord John Wenlock who, as a captain of Warwick's fleet, had helped in the capture of Richard Woodville at Sandwich 18 years before. Hawkins was put to the question and identified Sir Thomas Cooke, an Alderman high in the King's favour, as a secret supporter of Lancaster's cause.

Cooke was arrested and confined in the Tower; his wife was committed to the Mayor's custody until the case should be resolved. The King ordered that the hearing should be conducted by Justice Markham, known as "the upright judge", who would be assisted by the Duke of Clarence, the Earl of Warwick, and Richard Woodville, Earl Rivers. With unusual dedication to his duties, Rivers - who was "a great enemy" to the hapless Cooke - entered the now-unprotected town and country houses of the Alderman and diligently searched for papers which would prove his guilt. Although no such documentation was unearthed, Cooke's most valuable belongings somehow went missing during the search, including £1,600 worth of good woollen cloth which eventually found its way to a creditor of the King, Gerard Caniziani.

A verdict of High Treason on Cooke had been assumed to be a foregone conclusion by the Woodvilles and it came as a shock when Justice Markham directed the jury to find him guilty of the much lesser charge of misprision of treason, for which he was formally pardoned on July 26th. That, however, was far from the end of his troubles. Transferred from the Tower to the King's Bench Prison, he was eventually deprived of his position as Alderman by royal command on November 21st and obliged to pay a fine to the King of £8,000 before obtaining his freedom. Even then, his financial burdens were not over - Elizabeth Woodville issued a claim for Queen's Gold, an ancient custom whereby for every thousand pounds paid to the King, a hundred marks should, additionally, be paid to his consort. For a time Cooke refused to pay this last demand, but was eventually forced to comply, and to "compensate" the Queen's legal counsel as well, for the additional trouble he had caused them.

Cooke had maintained throughout the distasteful episode that his accuser, Hawkins, had come to him with a request for a loan of a thousand marks, which, it transpired was for Margaret of Anjou. When Cooke learned this he refused to make any loan and there, he had unwisely assumed, the matter ended. This version was later confirmed by Hawkins who, on the day of his execution, deposed that Cooke was entirely innocent of the charges he had made against him. Too late, alas, to prevent the gross injustice already done to Sir Thomas, whose real offence had been to incur the envy of Richard Woodville, his wife, Jacquetta and their daughter Elizabeth for his wealth. An innocent misdemeanour, but one which cost him dearly.

Nor was Cooke the only victim of the Woodville's spite, since Chief Justice Markham was subsequently removed from office on the insistence of the Queen, for jeopardising her father's grand scheme by insisting on a lesser verdict. Accounts of the evil-doings of the Queen and her family were spread widely by agents of the Earl of Warwick through the following twelve months, by which time Richard Neville's own grand design for redress of his wrongs was virtually completed, and another royal wedding was imminent.

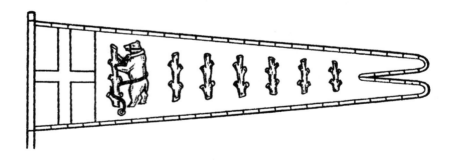

Standard of Richard Neville, Earl of Warwick

54

CHAPTER EIGHT

"So we, well-cover'd with the night's black mantle...may beat
down Edward's guard And seize himself..."
[Henry VI pt 3]

In April 1469, the Earl of Warwick, took his wife and daughters to Calais from where they were able to visit his cousin Margaret in her new Duchy of Burgundy and the Earl could have informal talks with her husband and inspect the fortifications at Calais, currently under the command of Warwick's Lieutenant, Lord John Wenlock. And, while he was conspicuously absent from England on family and the King's business, Richard Neville had left instructions for his carefully-laid plans to be implemented.

Through May and June, men were banding together all across the north of Yorkshire demanding redress of a variety of grievances and before the end of the month, a vast, unruly mob, 15,000 strong, stood before the walls of York demanding entrance. Unhappily for them, and their leader - a Robert Huldyard, masquerading as Robin of Redesdale - John Neville, Earl of Northumberland, was waiting inside the city with a strong, well-disciplined force and he sallied out and put the rebels to flight. Huldyard was taken and, with his customary zeal in the King's behalf, Neville had him publicly executed and his head displayed above the Micklegate Bar.

Warwick had returned to England when news of the rising reached him and was continuously with the King, reassuring him that the North was in good hands and that his presence would not be required so long as John Neville held the East March. Confirmation of this view was provided by news of events at York and with Warwick's encouragement, Edward left Windsor to make a tour he had long-planned through East Anglia, a part of his Kingdom noteworthy for its enduring support of the House of York. The King was accompanied by his brother, Richard of Gloucester, his old comrade-in-arms, Lord Hastings, and by his in-laws, Lords Rivers and Scales and Sir John Woodville. The party, having stayed at Bury St Edmunds, passed on to Norwich, where Edward enjoyed himself hugely and swore he would soon revisit and bring his wife with him. Then on to Lynn and Wisbech, making the traditional pilgrimage to Walsingham en route, and thence to Crowland and the ancient family home of the Yorks at Fotheringhay.

Here Elizabeth joined her husband and her father and brothers for what should have been a pleasant family reunion, but their contentment was short-lived as news continued to arrive of more, and much greater, upheaval in Yorkshire. A new Robin of Redesdale had emerged - some reports named him as Lord Robert Ogle, famed, battle-hardened Constable of Norham and a long-term adherent of the Middleham Nevilles, who was leading a disciplined army of 30,000 men south from the Humber with the declared purpose of laying their list of grievances before the King himself. Recognising that he had been misled as to the seriousness of the revolt, Edward swiftly - if belatedly - gathered what men were readily available and marched north. On July 9th, he sent out writs summoning his chief supporters to join him at Nottingham with all their force, meantime closing the city's gates and manning the walls against the approaching northerners.

Two of the King's principal magnates were not available to receive their summons. Days earlier, George, Duke of Clarence, and Richard Neville, Earl of Warwick, had slipped quietly and separately away to Calais where, on July 11th 1469, George Neville, Archbishop of York, united Clarence and his cousin, Isabel Neville, in wedlock. Then, his newly made son-in-law with him, Warwick sailed again for Kent with a strong force of men-at-arms and there published his prayer for redress of grievance, in terms identical to those being nailed to the door of every church in every northern town through which Redesdale's army was passing. Between the two burgeoning armies, Edward IV was caught in a trap made for him by his erstwhile mentor, the resurgent Earl of Warwick.

Warwick and Clarence moved quickly, via Canterbury, to London where the Mayor and Aldermen, with memories of Cooke's treatment still vivid in their minds, made the noble Lords greatly welcome and, by July 20th, Richard Neville with an army 20,000 strong was marching at steady pace towards St Albans and the road north. Ahead of them, Redesdale's army had reached Nottingham where Edward awaited their attack. To his surprise, however, the horde of rebels continued on their way southwards, clearly intent on linking with Warwick's army now advancing from London. When it became apparent Redesdale and his men had no intention of investing Nottingham, Edward decided to follow them. First, however, on the advice of his captains, he sent Rivers, Scales and John Woodville away, since he was told his troops would not fight to protect the lives of these men. Rivers quickly acquiesced in Edward's decision that they should depart before any fighting commenced and he, with his son John, moved to Grafton Regis, while Lord Scales rejoined the Queen at Norwich.

Edward then marched his army out of Nottingham, following, but keeping to the west of the Yorkshiremen's track, and edging southwards hoping to meet, and unite with, the contingents from Wales and the Westcountry led respectively by the new-made Earls of Pembroke and Devon, and which he knew were approaching. Unfortunately for him, and more so for them, they were met first by the larger army led by Robin of Redesdale in open hilly country a few miles northeast of Banbury near a tiny village called Edgecot.

Even more unhappily for the loyal forces, the day before had been marred by a blazing row between the respective leaders. William Herbert, Earl of Pembroke, had arrived first at Banbury and his 10,000 Welsh spearmen had filled all available billeting space. Weary after a day's forced marching, the Devon men - mainly archers - were obliged to turn south again and retrace their steps six miles to Deddington Castle, where they encamped for the night. Now, on July 26th, 1469, Herbert found himself about to face attack from a much-superior force with his nearest support marching miles to his rear and unlikely, after yesterday's events, to push forward very swiftly to his succour. But, Herbert was an experienced fighter, veteran of Mortimer's Cross, Towton and many another bloody skirmish in the Welsh Marches, and he placed his men on a very defensible piece of high ground commanding a level area called Dane's Moor across which the northern army was starting to advance. Before they engaged, Herbert sent couriers spurring back to the laggard Earl of Devon urging all possible haste if the reinforcement was to arrive in time.

The leaders of the Redesdale army were equally battle-wise and, seeing the loyal troops lacked bowmen, halted their own ranks and opened the attack with volleys of arrows mixed with hand-gun fire. Like the Lancastrian army at Towton, Herbert realised to stay on his ridge meant slow but certain defeat as his men were killed by long-range attack to which he had no means of replying and so he ordered his line to advance down on to the moor where the two armies came to grips. For a time, the Welshmen acquitted themselves well and several leaders of the rebels went down dead or badly hurt, including Robert Ogle whose wounds were to prove mortal. But the Yorkshiremen had the greater numbers and were suddenly reinforced by the arrival of Warwick's advance guard, led by another Towton veteran, John Clapham of Skipton, who had been attracted to the battle by the clamour of the conflict.

Clapham's charge into flank and rear proved too much for the gallant Welsh who broke and fled the field, meeting the advancing Devon men in their headlong flight and carrying them away with them. The rebels held the field and among their prisoners were the veteran Yorkist, Lord Herbert who, with his brother Richard, was executed the following morning, without formal trial, on the orders of Sir John Conyers, surviving commander of the rebels, and a close adherent of the Earl of Warwick.

Scouts from Warwick's army located the King, whose small army had melted away entirely as news of the defeat reached them at the small village of Olney, near Coventry, and George Neville, Archbishop of York, was sent with a strong force of heavily armed men to meet with and to escort Edward to his rendezvous with the master-planner who had brought about his downfall, Richard Neville, Earl of Warwick, maker - and unmaker - of Kings.

Edward and Warwick met again on July 31st and the King could not have been more amiable or helpful. Whatever the Earl wanted should be done and an initial wave of royal proclamations implementing the new policies went out on August 2nd, all impressed with King Edward's seal. Warwick, however, did not ask him to sign the warrants for the execution of Rivers and John Woodville who had been found in hiding at their manor of Grafton and were conducted thence to Northampton. There on August 12th, 1469, died Richard Woodville, once the handsomest man in England, whose good looks and debonair ways had made him the lover, and then husband, of a wealthy Burgundian Princess, by whom he had 15 children, most of them surviving him, and all of them handsome, greedy and feckless. His son John, husband of the ancient Dowager Duchess of Norfolk, who was also aunt to the Earl of Warwick, followed him under the headsman's axe.

Four other sons survived him and all eight of his daughters, of whom the eldest was Queen of England and one who, with her widowed mother, would not rest until a full blood-price had been paid for the dead Woodville men. And though the King might smile and acquiesce in whatever twist or turn in policy the Earl of Warwick put to him and assure his captor of his perfect happiness to be immured in Warwick Castle or later in Middleham Keep, wherever his captor might deem best, he had marked the great Earl for death. Now, it was merely a matter of time.

CHAPTER NINE

"...the people, seeing their king detained as a prisoner, refused
to take any notice of proclamations..."
[Crowland Chronicle Second Continuation]

While the fortunes of her family were enduring such tragic reverses and the very safety of her husband was brought into question by the successful coup of the Earl of Warwick, Elizabeth Woodville, Queen of England, was enjoying a royal progress through East Anglia. In mid-July, while great armies were converging from north and south and west, her party was in Norfolk, visiting several of the towns where her husband had been made so welcome during the Spring of the year and enjoying an extended stay in Norwich - which Edward had particularly commended for its hospitality - and where the Queen now enjoyed feasting and singing and masquers performing pageants for her royal pleasure.

However, all the merriment was brought to a sudden halt by the arrival of her brother Anthony, Lord Scales, with unwelcome news of the great rebellion and the resulting peril to the King's rule, and quite possibly to his life. Even while they considered their safest course of action, news arrived from Edgecot of the defeat of the loyalist forces there and the deaths of Lord Herbert and his brother. Clearly, the rebels were in the ascendant and the safest place for the Queen, her attendants and her brother was London, where Edward, and the House of York's popularity should provide assurance of security until firmer tidings of the King's whereabouts and his own safety arrived.

It was at Westminster, therefore, that on July 31st, Queen Elizabeth and her mother received the sad news of the deaths of Richard and John Woodville and of the effective imprisonment of King Edward by the Earl of Warwick. At the same time, insult was added to injury by a formal accusation of witchcraft against the newly widowed Jacquetta, who was alleged, by a man called Thomas Wake, to have employed sorcery in bringing King Edward to marry her daughter. Perhaps Wake spoke truer than he knew, though any "sorcery" used by Jacquetta of Luxembourg in captivating the young King was as old as the Garden of Eden and not punishable by burning. However that may be, the accusation was quashed as groundless in space of a few months, but its hurt left lasting mental scars on mother and on daughter.

By late August, Edward had been transferred to Middleham and, from here, he continued to sign and seal the proclamations of governance as set out by Warwick. Nevertheless, the Earl sensed that control of the Kingdom was somehow slipping from his grasp and decided that an Act of Parliament was needed to establish the new regime. The Estates were summoned to meet in York on September 20th, but the projected assembly was aborted by events. As had happened so many times in the previous twenty years, the lack of firm, central Authority in England had led on to anarchy and, while Warwick might issue his writs from Middleham, the mob was out in London pillaging the wealthy and driving out foreign merchants; Howards and Pastons in East Anglia and Berkeleys and Talbots in the West country feuded and fought. The final blow came when Humphrey Neville of the family's Westmorland branch came over the Border with a strong band of Scots and proceeded to ravage the northern counties while calling for the restoration of Lancaster.

John Neville was unable to raise sufficient levies to deal with the threat from the north and Warwick was obliged to ask the King for his support in this essential recruitment. Edward indicated his entire willingness to help, but suggested that his proclamations to this end would be more effective if they came from a King clearly free to make his own decisions and express his own will. In short, it might be better if Edward were to move away from Middleham to, say, the royal demesne at Pontefract and to issue the summons to arms from there. Warwick had little alternative but to agree and Edward moved to south Yorkshire, the writs were issued and recruits flocked to Montagu's banner. Reinforced, John Neville had little trouble in putting down the rebellion and sending the Scots packing back over the Border. Their former leader, Humphrey Neville, who had escaped with his life on several similar occasions previously, finally ran out of luck and was publicly executed at York, in the presence of his King, on September 29th.

Shortly afterwards, Richard of Gloucester and Lord William Hastings arrived at Pontefract castle at the head of 2,000 well-armed men to escort the King back to his palace of Westminster. Warwick was powerless to prevent this resumption of power and, in the remaining months of 1469, Edward undid much of what his cousin had achieved during his enforced captivity. Among his earliest moves was confirmation of Anthony Woodville, Lord Scales, as the second Earl Rivers, clear evidence of the resurgent powers of the Queen and her mother. Again, the sun was shining on the fortunes of the Woodvilles. And then Edward made a mistake. He fashioned a two-pronged move to break the Neville power in the north and to separate John Neville from his familial loyalties. Unfortunately for him, for his realm and for the many men who would die as a result, he did not think to ask John Neville whether he agreed with his King's gambit.

His recent experiences as a captive - however comfortable that captivity might have been made - and the ruthless brutality evident in Warwick's summary disposal of the Herberts and of Richard and John Woodville had made clear to Edward that steps must be taken to neutralise the power of the Nevilles in the north of his Kingdom. He could do little about Warwick's main power-base at Middleham, but the East March was a different matter. The Percy family had held sway there for centuries past and the present interruption in their rule had lasted for only the eight years which had elapsed since the death of the third Earl at Towton. His son had been lodged in the Tower since his father's demise and his inheritance given to John Neville as reward for his victory at Hexham five years earlier. But the loyalties of Northumberland folk were still, first and foremost, to the Percies and Edward would take advantage of that important factor.

In October, the young Harry Percy was released from the Tower and the month following, John Neville was told by Edward that in recognition of his long and faithful service he would become Marquis Montagu and, while he would lose the Earldom of Northumberland, he would receive equivalent properties in the south and south-west, much of his new estate coming from the confiscated lands of the Courtenays. Further, his son George would be betrothed to Edward's oldest child and apparent heir, Elizabeth, and would be made Duke of Bedford, so that he should have sufficient status for the effective position of co-heir to the throne of England. A glittering prospect indeed for the Montagu branch of the Middleham Nevilles - it was unfortunate that John Neville should have fallen in love with his identity as Earl of Northumberland, and the new Marquis - ever a quiet man - saw no useful purpose to be served in drawing such a minor point to the attention of his royal master.

On March 1st, 1470, Henry Percy was installed as fourth Earl of Northumberland - the Neville interregnum was brief enough to be ignored - and he and his people played little or no part in the stirring events which would again convulse England during the coming year, nor in the things to come, when Percy's lack of support for his King on a hill in Leicestershire, would see the final overthrow of the House of Plantagenet. But, for now, a Percy was master in Alnwick again and Warwick's writ no longer ran on the eastern Border. Richard Neville could see the way the wind was blowing and determined that it was probably time for the heirs of Robin of Redesdale to make a further appearance on the stage of history.

The Earl of Warwick was a complex man and his ability to manoeuvre politically and diplomatically was unsurpassed in his time. Only Louis XI, the Spider King of France, was a match for Richard Neville's talents in this field, and both men infinitely preferred to achieve their ends by these methods, rather than to engage in bloody warfare. Direct violence was not a strong point of either. Accordingly, when Warwick started again to plot treason, which, this time, should involve the final downfall of Edward IV, the resulting plan was complicated in the extreme and missed two obvious, potential shortcomings: too great a reliance on untried henchmen and an over-simplistic belief that Edward could be caught twice in the same trap.

This time, the plot was launched by Lord Richard Welles, who was related by marriage to Warwick's liegeman, Sir James Strangways, and who was involved in a long-term feud with Sir Thomas Burgh of Gainsborough. Sir Thomas was Edward's chief supporter in Lincolnshire and any attack on him would be seen as an assault on the King's own authority, which Edward must surely answer. In February 1470 therefore, Lord Welles' son, Sir Robert, led "riotous bands" to pillage Burgh's estates and attack and plunder his Manor House, all in the cause of protest against the King's misgovernance. And during these events, the Duke of Clarence was living quietly in his London mansion, while the Earl of Warwick tended his own estates in Warwickshire.

Edward saw clearly the pit which had been dug for him and, on this occasion, wasted no time in pleasurable dalliance. Instead, he sent fast couriers spurring north with safe conducts to Lord Welles and his brother-in-law Sir Thomas Dymmock, summoning both to attend him in London immediately to answer for the deeds of their men. Simultaneously, the King sent out commissions of array to selected Lords, including Warwick and Clarence, requiring them all to raise armed bands and to join the royal force at Grantham on March 12th.

Welles and Dymmock responded promptly to the King's summons and assured Edward that they deplored equally the actions of Sir Robert Welles and that proper reparation would be made for the harm done to Sir Thomas Burgh's property. The King readily acquitted both men of blame, but, despite the safe-conducts he had sent to them, kept the two knights with him as possible bargaining counters in the coming confrontation with Robert Welles. Meantime, the Earl of Warwick had written to Edward confirming receipt of the commission of array and saying he would meet with the King, as commanded, at Grantham on March 12th, and had also written secretly to Robert Welles telling him to bring his rebels to Leicester on the same date, there to rendezvous with him and Clarence. In this way, their combined force would lie between the King and his capital and Edward would be caught again between Warwick's anvil and the hammer from north Yorkshire, where Sir John Conyers and other Middleham adherents were already gathering their men.

Edward, moving with all his former speed and firmness of purpose, was at Stamford with a very substantial force of men on March 11th and his scouts located the Lincolnshire rebels some five miles north of the town, moving to cross Ermine Street, towards their Leicester meeting-place. Edward immediately sent heralds to Robert Welles ordering him to disband his forces and surrender himself to his King's grace on pain of his father's death. Sir Robert sent a temporising reply to the King and other messengers to Warwick saying that he must confront Edward to rescue his father. The rebels then moved southwards, away from any possible support from the master-planner to meet the royal army. Richard Neville's schemes were fast unravelling.

Robert Welles met the King's army near the village of Empingham and arrayed his men in battle lines. Edward summoned him to surrender and when he again refused, his father and uncle were led out between the two armies and beheaded without more ado. This pitiless deed started panic in the ranks of the rebels which was immediately exacerbated by cannonades from the great guns Edward had brought with him and general rout ensued when the King himself led the charge on the disorganised ranks before him. The main killing ground was a large copse of trees immediately to the right rear of the rebel line and known ever after as Bloody Oaks. The Lincolnshire rebellion was over.

Sir Robert Welles was captured at Doncaster within a few days of the collapse of the revolt and was beheaded there after making a full confession implicating Warwick and Clarence as the secret leaders of the uprising. The two had moved north to Chesterfield, following news of Welles' defeat at Empingham, in order to be closer to their hoped-for reinforcements from north Yorkshire. However, Edward saw to it that news of the end of the uprising and its bloody consequences were widely published throughout the county and himself reached York on March 21st, where he received the submission of Conyers and Warwick's other supporters. Richard Neville and his son-in-law Clarence moved south again to Warwick Castle where they collected their families and moved on towards the coast and Calais.

Warwick was again disappointed when he reached his looked-for haven on the French coast, since his erstwhile Lieutenant, Lord John Wenlock, who had received his King's commands before the Earl's arrival, refused him entry to the port and backed this with a warning broadside from his cannon. Deprived of his former base, Warwick moved on to Honfleur, the traditional landing point for English fleets and from there, on May 1st, 1470 he sent word to Louis of France that the support and services of the now-landless Earl of Warwick were at his disposal.

Ancient Arms of France,
- the "fleurs-de-lis".

CHAPTER TEN

"...the queen persevered for fifteen days ere she would anything
intend to the said treaty of marriage...."

[Chronicles of the White Rose]

With Warwick fled to the last refuge still open to him, Edward and his Queen gave thanks for the restoration of peace in their realm with a magnificent celebration of the Feast of Pentecost at Canterbury. Edward arrived there on June 6th, followed two days later by his Queen and their oldest daughter, the princess Elizabeth. The royal party was received at the door of the Abbey by monks in white vestments, led by their Prior, John Oxney, and all entered the seat of Saint Augustine to give thanks for the King's victory. The following day, Saturday, the nobility of Laity and Church arrived, notable among them Earl Rivers, the Queen's brother, and the Earl of Worcester, John Tiptoft, who was fast earning a reputation as the Queen's "enforcer", and a cruel one by all accounts, with the Bishops of Bangor, Carlisle, Durham and Ely and many other dignitaries.

The day following was Whitsuntide and Edward and Elizabeth led the great procession at High Mass, which was celebrated by the Bishop of Rochester, one Thomas Rotherham, who as Archbishop of York and Chancellor of England would figure largely in events to come twelve years later, when many of his co-celebrants were dead. In particular, Elizabeth Woodville would have cause to rue the longevity - and indecisiveness - of the former Bishop of Rochester. The following day, King and Queen attended High Mass and Vespers together, and afterwards, Edward went on to the Kentish coast to inspect the fortifications at Sandwich and Dover and thence back to London to rejoin his wife and family. Life was good and peaceful in the England of the Summer of 1470, but a cloud no bigger than the hand of the King of France was gathering on the eastern horizon.

Richard Neville, George of Clarence and their families were not the only distinguished exiles from England at the court of France. For seven years, Margaret of Anjou and her son, Edward of Lancaster, Prince of Wales had eked out a sorry existence dependent utterly on the charity of Louis XI, a ruler not famed for generosity, indeed, some said, a miserly monarch, wearing lead badges in his hat rather than silver and old gowns well-stained with food and wine droppings. With no other support available to her, Queen Margaret's lot had been far from happy and the chief blame for all her degradation she laid firmly at the door of Richard Neville, Earl of Warwick and Salisbury, the wealthiest Peer in England, who through his scheming had reduced his rightful Queen to utter penury. The thought of, one day, paying Warwick out in his own coin had kept her alive through the years of struggle and banishment and she was able to rejoice now that, while her own case might not be improved, at least the mighty Earl had come down to the same level.

Then, as the high days of Summer passed, messengers came from Louis, inviting Margaret and her tattered court to spend some time with him in more pleasant surroundings. This the Queen was happy to do, since, if naught else, it would give her an opportunity to talk to Louis about the sore need for an increase in the small pension he allowed her and permit her and her followers to live at the King's expense for a short while. When she arrived, the politesses were got quickly out of the way and Louis of France wasted little time in coming to his point. He had been talking with Warwick and Clarence and felt they might be amenable to allying their fortunes with those of Lancaster and restoring Henry VI to the throne of England. How would Queen Margaret feel about such a joining?

Margaret's first - and furious - reaction was to reject the idea out of hand, but she was dealing with the master-diplomat of his age. Gradually, Louis talked her around to his way of thinking and, at last, with stern provisos on a grovelling, public submission to her from Warwick, and proper financial provision for herself and her court from then on, and with all the risk to life and limb to be borne by Warwick, the deal was done. Henry VI should be restored, his son Edward would be his heir apparent and would marry Anne Neville, Warwick's younger daughter, to seal the bargain. George of Clarence, previously heir to King Edward IV, by virtue of Elizabeth Woodville's continuing failure to produce a son, would be heir-presumptive, unless and until Edward and Anne produced a closer successor.

All the parties to the arrangement were happy with what had been achieved, with the exception of the Duke of Clarence. At a stroke, he had lost half his potential claim to the vast estates of the Earl of Warwick and his right of succession to the English throne had, effectively, been nullified. And, as all this disappointment sank into his consciousness, George of Clarence received the first missive in what would become a developing clandestine

Louis XI, King of France.

(Portrait at Plessy les tours from an original by Jean Fouqett)

correspondence with his brothers, Edward and Richard, his mother, Cecily, Duchess of York, and his sisters including Margaret, the new Duchess of Burgundy. The Duke found himself under pressure, from both sides, to return to his familial loyalties, but, before he could make up his mind, his decision was overtaken by events and, with his father-in-law and a substantial French-financed force, he found himself landing at Plymouth as co-leader of a host calling for the restoration of Henry VI to the throne of England.

During July there had been regular reports of growing unrest in north Yorkshire as Warwick's agents and adherents stirred up trouble. By the end of the month, Edward learned that Lord Fitzhugh, Warwick's brother-in-law, was raising the standard of revolt and was being joined by large numbers of the commons. He placed Elizabeth, pregnant with her fourth child, and their three daughters in the Tower for safe-keeping and, on August 5th, marched northwards with as many men as he could quickly raise to confront Fitzhugh. The King made York his main base and there he was soon busy issuing pardons to surrendering rebels, the rising have died quickly once the warrior-king arrived. However, Fitzhugh's rebellion had served its real purpose very well, for it was at York, on September 25th, that Edward received news of Warwick's landing, 12 days previously and 300 miles to the south. Once more, it seemed, the wily Earl of Warwick had caught his King at a disadvantage.

Decisive as always when danger was greatest, Edward broke camp and marched out of the city, southwards, to confront the returned Richard Neville. Royal couriers were sent spurring to Pontefract, where John Neville, the new Marquis Montagu, commanded, and the main northern body of Edward's men was garrisoned, ordering him to bring with him all the troops he had and to rendezvous with the King at Doncaster. Resting there for the night of September 26th, Edward was awakened by news of an approaching enemy force and while not believing the first reports, he was soon made aware, by fleeing deserters, that the oncoming "enemy" was in fact Montagu, who had declared for Warwick and Lancaster, and was leading 6,000 troops westwards towards Doncaster.

Faced with this disastrous news and knowing that Warwick was already encamped at Coventry with, reportedly, 30,000 men at his back, Edward realised the game was lost and, ordering his own small force to disperse, he set out for Norfolk with only a small bodyguard and his brother Richard, Lord Hastings and Anthony Woodville, Earl Rivers, who had no doubt what his own fate would be if he were taken by Warwick. After narrowly escaping drowning in the Wash, the party reached Lynn on September 29th and set out three days later for the doubtful welcome awaiting them from the Duke of Burgundy. Edward landed at Alkmaar without money or arms but was fortunate enough to encounter almost immediately, Louis de Gruthuyse, Governor of Holland, who had formed a personal friendship with King Edward some years previously while on a visit to England. Gruthuyse now gave Edward and his small band hospitality and funds, and then conducted them to the Hague where they arrived on October 12th.

Meantime, in London, news had reached Elizabeth Woodville of Warwick's return and there were many rumours of the vast army he had brought with him and the number of Lancastrians rallying to his banner when it was proclaimed that he had come to re-install the rightful King on his throne. Waiting for news from her husband, she ordered the Constable of the Tower to bring in supplies and to prepare the fortress to withstand siege if necessary. However, when messengers from Edward finally arrived, their only tidings were of the disaster which had overtaken him and his following flight to the uncertain refuge of Burgundy.

Panicking, the Queen abandoned all thought of standing firm in the Tower and on the night of October 1st, with her children and her mother, Jacquetta, she took boat and moved up-river to Westminster where she debarked and registered her party at the Abbey as Sanctuary-women. Using the Abbot as a go-between, Elizabeth advised the Lord Mayor, Richard Lee, that she desired to surrender her late refuge to him and his Aldermen, lest the Kentishmen should invade the City to despoil and kill the inhabitants. On October 3rd, the City fathers duly took formal possession of the Tower in the name of King Henry, who, for years past, had been its most closely-guarded tenant. Immediately afterwards, a proclamation was issued in Henry's name ordering, on pain of death, that there should be no despoiling of churches or sanctuaries, which did much to reassure the Woodville women as to their personal safety in Westminster.

The Earl of Warwick wasted little time in taking over the reins of Government and, among the early orders and appointments issued by the royal Council was one to Lady Scrope, commanding her to wait on Elizabeth, whose confinement was known to be approaching. She was further comforted by a number of small gifts sent to her by the Abbot, Thomas Milling, while a butcher, John Gould, agreed to provide her and her household with half a steer and two sheep a week for their sustenance. When her labour commenced,

Marjorie Cobb, her regular midwife was allowed to enter the sanctuary to attend her, as was her physician, Master Serigo and, on November 2nd 1470, at the nadir of York and Woodville fortunes, was born a boy, who was speedily and unceremoniously baptised Edward, by the sub-prior of the Abbey, with Thomas Milling, his Prior John Esteney, and Lady Scrope standing as Godparents.

No note was taken of the birth by the Earl of Warwick or his Council, but it was said by some, who looked for the return of his father one day, that this arrival of a male heir was a happy omen.

Representation of Richard Neville in full armour.

(Geoffrey Wheeler)

CHAPTER ELEVEN

"...I like not this flight of Edward's; For doubtless Burgundy will yield him help And we shall have more wars before't be long..."

[Henry VI pt 3]

In November 1470, the Earl of Warwick summoned a Parliament to Westminster which passed a mass of legislation legalising the return of Lancaster to power in England. Long-standing attainders on Lancastrian supporters were reversed and replaced by similar proscription of the Yorkist leaders, in particular Edward, now-styled Duke of York and Richard, Duke of Gloucester. The final and possibly most significant Act of the session agreed a treaty of peace and friendship with France and on the 28th of the month at Amboise, Edward of Lancaster, Prince of Wales, formally signed an Alliance with Louis of France agreeing English support for his war against Charles of Burgundy. The first instalment of Louis' price for the restoration of Lancaster had been quickly and cheaply paid - settlement of the balance would cost England much blood and France much treasure.

With a joyful Christmastide passed in peace and a more prosperous 1471 in prospect, Richard Neville, Earl of Warwick and undoubted Ruler of England, had good reason to feel satisfied with the change in his fortunes over the previous year. But, his apple was not entirely without its share of worms. Louis XI was pressing him for action against Burgundy in support of the renewed French campaign and was growing increasingly impatient with Warwick's response that he dared not leave England without a firm hand on the tiller of the ship of state, which meant that Margaret of Anjou and her son must return to govern the land through her husband. For her part, however, Queen Margaret was understandably hesitant to risk life and fortune again in a land which had always seemed foreign to her and for whose people, with few exceptions, she felt little but abhorrence, a feeling which was entirely reciprocated. And, she would never feel entirely secure until Edward of York was cold in his grave.

Unlike Queen Margaret, Charles of Burgundy had done with

hesitation. When he heard of the Treaty signing at Amboise, he sent word to his brother-in-law that they should meet to discuss developments and the two met, first at Aire on January 2nd and five days later had further discussion at St Pol, where Edward was staying with Jacquetta's brother, Jacques of Luxembourg. Following the talks Charles gave out that no help should be given to the Yorkist party, but secretly lent Edward fifty thousand florins, with which to hire mercenary troops and re-equip his own men, and provided a small fleet of more than a dozen vessels for transportation of the party to England, as and when Edward of York was ready to move. However, the Duke of Burgundy hoped the departure would not be long delayed, since the long-threatened juncture between Warwick's army and the Host of France appeared imminent.

For some weeks, Edward found the weather too foul for seafaring and had to tramp the wharves at Flushing, bridling his impatience to be back in England as best he could. Fortunately for Burgundy, the same storms also kept Warwick's fleet port-bound, but, as the weather finally broke, Richard Neville prepared to move his army out of London towards Sandwich where they would embark for Calais, and sent word to Louis that he would be with him before the month was out. Unhappily for both rulers, Warwick received word from his coast-watchers on March 12th that a fleet flying Yorkist banners had been sighted off Cromer in Norfolk, but had failed to land there and had continued northwards, clearly seeking a landing-site. This they found, traditionally, at Ravenspur, in the Humber's mouth, and here, on March 14th, 1471, Edward, Richard, Hastings and 2,000 men disembarked as Henry Bolingbroke had done 70 years earlier.

The news reached Warwick on the 16th, by which time he was already moving north with his force towards Coventry, summoning friends and allies to join him there with all the power they could raise. In particular, he sent to his brother John, Marquis Montagu, that he should move against Edward from his Pontefract base as quickly as possible and delay any move southwards until Warwick should have gathered an overwhelming force. This Montagu tried to do but found his recruiting efforts were rendered largely vain through the activities of Harry Percy, restored Earl of Northumberland, who did nothing to hamper the movements of his benefactor. This enabled Edward to enter York on March 18th, where - again, emulating Bolingbroke - he proclaimed that he came only for his dukedom. He gathered more men and moved south, sending word to his wife and family of his impending return and secretly to his brother, George of Clarence, telling him to bring all the force he could muster to meet his brothers' army to the south of Warwick.

Slipping past Montagu, who felt he had insufficient force to stop the King's onward march, feinting at John de Vere and Exeter who scurried away to join Warwick at Coventry and then, after challenging Richard Neville to single combat before the walls of Coventry, Edward, once more now claiming Kingship over England, found Clarence at Banbury with 4,000 well-armed men and their combined force moved speedily to London. There the citizens gave them hearty welcome and Edward hastened to Westminster to be reunited with his wife and his family, and to see for the first time his son and heir. Now he had a dynasty to establish and fight for and he bent all his efforts to enlisting a force strong enough to overthrow the united power of Neville and Lancaster, which he knew was already moving to meet him.

He took his family out of the Sanctuary of the Abbey and moved them instead to his mother's house, Baynard's Castle within the city walls, on Maundy Thursday and here he and his Queen heard evening mass together and kept Good Friday. The following day, Edward moved out of London leading 10,000 men northwards to meet the approaching Warwick, and his outriders found the Earl arrayed for battle across a low ridge to the north of a village called Barnet. The evening shadows were lengthening as the army of King Edward, led by the young Duke of Gloucester making his first fight, moved into battle formation facing Warwick's position and the two forces settled in their lines for the night. The long-drawn out struggle between Edward and his mightiest Lord would be decided, finally and ironically, on the Anniversary of the Resurrection.

Fighting began at daybreak on Sunday, April 14th, 1471 with, as Warwick and Montagu had anticipated, Edward - despite a thick swirling mist which hid each side from the other - moving forward with his whole force to the attack. The Lancastrian army had orders to stand fast and let the Yorkist tide wear itself out on the steel-clad lines facing them, but their right wing was commanded by the warlike John de Vere, Earl of Oxford, and as soon as he heard the clash of arms begin he ordered his line to attack to their front. Due to a maladjustment of their formation, the opposing forces outflanked each other on the right wing of the army and, with this advantage, Oxford quickly broke the division facing him, commanded by Lord Hastings, and put them to flight with de Vere himself leading the pursuit.

Montagu who commanded the Lancastrian centre against Edward, did not see the break-through by his right, due to the thick fog and, equally, Edward and his centre division were unaware that their left flank was "in the air" and unguarded. In blissful ignorance, the two continued their own combat à l'outrance. Montagu's left flank was covered by Henry Holland, Duke of Exeter, who quickly found his division in the same parlous position as Hastings before him, with Richard of Gloucester outflanking him and pushing his division back and back despite his constant calls on the reserve division, commanded by Warwick himself, for replacements and reinforcement. Montagu, likewise, continually adjusted his own line to conform with Exeter's retreating division and by late morning, when the sun at last began to burn off the mist, the whole battle-line had swung through 90 degrees.

Thus, when Oxford, having realised there was still fighting to be done before the day was won, collected his division again and turned from pursuing Hastings to charge into what had been the flank and rear of Edward's division, he found himself attacking Montagu's right wing. John Neville's men, surprised initially by this onset, rallied quickly and fired volleys of arrows into de Vere's troops, mistaking, in the partial mist still prevailing, de Vere's Shooting Star banner for Edward's Sun in Splendour. Oxford's men, realising that it was Montagu's archers who were firing into their line, assumed that their previous unease about alliance with former Yorkist foes had been well justified, and raising the familiar cry of "Treason" quickly quit the field. Their intervention, however, had wrought its mischief on Montagu's division which began to recoil from Edward's hard pounding attack and the King, master battlefield general, sensing the weakening to his front, redoubled his efforts and, with Gloucester successful on the right flank, Warwick's army broke up and ran.

The great Earl was caught by swift-running archers as he lumbered in full armour towards the sanctuary of the horse-lines and swiftly despatched. John, Marquis Montagu, continued his losing battle to the end and died on the field with his men. The bodies of both were found, stripped, and taken back to London where they were displayed in open coffins, outside St Paul's, with only their loins being covered. Thus London could see that the King's chief enemies were dead; thus could Elizabeth Woodville rejoice in a just retribution visited on the man who had killed her father and her brother.

Edward and his army made a triumphal re-entry into London, but had little time to celebrate their victory. Two days later came news that Margaret of Anjou and her son Edward, Prince of Wales, had landed at Weymouth and joined Edmund Beaufort, Duke of Somerset who was rousing the west country yet again in the cause of Lancaster. The King's army marched out of London on April 17th, with Richard of Gloucester leading the vanguard and Hastings the rear. After much marching and counter-marching, the last army of Lancaster was located at Bristol on May 2nd, but Beaufort - a more skilful general than former holders of his title - slipped past Edward's battle-array and marched northwards towards the succour of the Welsh hills and the reinforcement offered by Jasper Tudor, former Earl of Pembroke.

Edward caught his enemies, short of the Severn crossing, on May 4th, at Tewkesbury and there, despite a brilliant outflanking manoeuvre by Somerset which was thwarted by the dogged courage of Richard of Gloucester, King Edward IV crushed the old enemy's forlorn hope and Lancaster went down to final defeat. Edward Prince of Wales died on the field, Somerset - hauled out of Sanctuary in Tewkesbury Abbey - received summary justice by the headsman's axe on the following day, and the former Queen Margaret was taken in flight at Coventry on May 7th. She suffered imprisonment until ransomed five years later by Louis of France as part of his "Dane-geld" peace treaty with Edward and her life ended as a poor pensioner at the French court at the age of 52. She died, some said, of a broken heart,

Having moved with his victorious train from Worcester to take possession of his Queenly prisoner, Edward was surprised on May 14th to receive urgent messages from Queen Elizabeth that she and all his family were in peril of their lives, besieged in the Tower by the Bastard of Fauconberg, son of William Neville, late Earl of Kent, who had led Edward's archers at Towton. The King immediately despatched a force of 1,500 men to reinforce the London garrison and followed himself two days later with the bulk of his army.

Fauconberg had been unable to force a crossing of the Thames and burned London Bridge, before being caught by a sortie from the Tower garrison led, it was reported, by Anthony Woodville, Earl Rivers, and driven away from the capital. Hearing of Edward's imminent arrival, he withdrew back into Kent. Here he was caught by the King's men and suffered a traitor's death of hanging, drawing and quartering four months later. His rebellion, in the end, had done little more than provide England's undoubted King with the opportunity, on May 21st, for another triumphal entry into his capital city and a further excuse, if one were needed, for the final elimination of the House of Lancaster. On Edward's orders, Henry VI, last and weakest of the three Lancastrian Kings, was killed in his apartment at the Tower that very night. So ended the dynasty, founded by John of Gaunt, third son of Edward III, which had ruled England for more than 70 years.

Elizabeth Woodville.

(Detail from Queen's College, Cambridge portrait)

CHAPTER TWELVE

"Sound drums and trumpets. Farewell, sour annoy !
For here, I hope, begins our lasting joy. "

[Henry VI pt 3]

A month after the death of Henry VI, Edward began to provide for the establishment of his own dynasty. On June 26th, his son Edward, then aged seven months, was created Prince of Wales. Two weeks later, the King issued letters patent creating a Council with "large power" to advise and counsel the young Prince, of which Clarence and Gloucester were members, together with leaders of the Church, the Queen, and her brother Anthony, Earl Rivers. In September, the King and Queen made a further pilgrimage to Canterbury, where thank-offerings for his victories were laid and it was said that never before had so many people been seen in pilgrimage together.

At Christmas, the King and Queen had a crowning ceremony at Westminster and on New Year's Day and the Twelfth Day of Christmas, the royal couple again processed magnificently to the Abbey and myriad onlookers could see that the Queen was again great with child. In February 1472, Edward and Elizabeth went to Sheen where the King hoped to reconcile his brothers. Richard was intent on marrying Anne Neville, widow of Edward of Lancaster, and co-heiress with her sister to the enormous wealth of the Warwick Earldom, Clarence opposed the match, to the length of hiding the intended bride, disguised as a maid, in a friend's kitchens, and furiously refused to part with any of the Warwick inheritance.

Thanks to Edward's mediation, Clarence eventually and grudgingly consented to the marriage and agreed that Richard should have Middleham and some other holdings in north Yorkshire, but insisted on keeping the bulk of the estate for himself. By the end of Spring, the newly-weds were established in their home in Middleham's Keep, where both had spent the happiest years of their childhood, and, on April 19th, Elizabeth had given birth to another daughter, Margaret, while in residence at Windsor. The early Summer of 1472 promised well for the House of York.

On May 30th, however, tragedy struck. The Duchess of Bedford,

Jacquetta of Luxembourg, apt descendant of Melusine, the water nymph of Lusignan, whose beauty and joie de vivre had captivated Kings and great Lords and "the handsomest man in England", now in her mid-fifties, died. Her spirit, her beauty and her burning ambition had fired the Commoner family into which she had wed, with an untoward pride and a hunger for greatness which would prove insatiable and cost them, and her adopted country, dear in gold and blood. But, for now, Elizabeth the Queen, her brothers and sisters, and her children mourned the passing of a great lady.

By September, the grieving was over and, for a week, there was feasting, dancing and merriment at Edward's court for the visit of Louis de Gruthuyse who had welcomed the exiled King on his arrival in Burgundy two years earlier. Edward took Louis into his family and lavished gifts upon him, including a great cup of gold decorated with pearls. In the bowl was set a piece of Unicorn's horn - a specific against any poison inserted into the cup - and on the cover was a great sapphire. The celebrations reached their climax on October 13th when de Gruthuyse attended a gathering in the Parliament chamber and was created Earl of Winchester. The following day, the new Earl took ship back to Holland, his friendship for the House of York and its leader strongly reinforced.

By the end of 1472, Edward had granted the infant Prince of Wales a separate household which would be located in the Yorkist heartland of the Marches at Ludlow. Elizabeth took her son there in February, 1473 and with him went his Uncle Anthony Woodville, Earl Rivers whom Edward had happily granted his wife's request to install as his son's chief Governor during his infancy. The boy's Chamberlain and tutor, Thomas Vaughan, who had carried the tiny Prince in the processions honouring the Earl of Winchester and was a life-long retainer of the Woodville family, also went with the household. Clearly, the future King of England was destined to be strongly influenced by his maternal family.

King Edward visited his young son in June of the year and from Ludlow, he travelled across the region, visiting Coventry, Leicester and Kenilworth showing himself to his people and meeting with the local magnates. In August, he moved to Shrewsbury to be with Queen Elizabeth during her imminent confinement and here, on the 17th of the month, a second son was born, Richard of Shrewsbury, soon to be created Duke of York. Continuation of the Plantagenet dynasty into a fourth century seemed now to be assured.

Intent on her own family increasing its wealth and power, so that it might share fully in the benefits flowing from the uninterrupted rule of the House of York, Elizabeth Woodville had been seeking, for some time, a suitable match for her oldest son by her first marriage, Thomas Grey. His first bride, Anne Holland, heiress to the Duke of Exeter, "stolen" from young George Neville, son of Montagu, by a 4,000 mark bribe from the Queen to Anne's mother in 1466 had died little more than a year later and a seven year widowhood was unduly long in those times. So it was that, in the mid-Summer of 1474, arrangements were finally concluded for the marriage of Thomas Grey, now Earl of Huntingdon, stepson to King Edward, to Cecily Bonville - Baroness Bonville in her own right - and daughter of Katherine Neville, who, following the death of Lord Bonville, her first husband, at Wakefield had subsequently married William, Lord Hastings, the King's most loyal friend.

The match brought fresh accumulation of wealth and lands to the Woodville family and, to ensure its safe retention, the wedding settlement was drawn up in the Summer Parliament and the doting King agreed that two unusual clauses should be included. First, in the event of Thomas's death, ownership of all the estates accruing to the family by the marriage would revert to his younger brother Richard Grey. Second, the total income from Cecily's fortune for two years after the wedding - the bride was only twelve years of age - should be paid to the Queen and her assignees. Amongst the latter was Hastings, who received 2,500 marks for the marriage. And, a final wedding gift from the King's bounty, on April 18th, 1475, Thomas Grey was created Marquess of Dorset. The rapacity of Elizabeth Woodville in advancing her family's fortunes was boundless and caused ever-increasing jealousy and dislike of these parvenu descendants of "a knave's son" and "a common squire". In particular, the dissatisfaction of George, Duke of Clarence had reached boiling point and his hatred of the Queen and all her kin would make itself apparent in early course and make mock of his brother's hoped-for "lasting joy".

For much of the year prior to Dorset's elevation to his new eminence, the King had been preoccupied with raising funds, allegedly to reassert the Plantagenets' ancient claim to the throne of France. In this task, he was greatly helped by John Morton, his Master of the Rolls, who was proving himself as adept at developing new systems of taxation as he had in developing an original system for storing the files of the King's Council. By the July of 1475, Edward had his funding and his recruits and landed at Calais with 1,500 men-at-arms and 15,000 archers. Louis, the Spider King of France, had no wish to try conclusions with the mighty warrior-king of the English and, since there was no sign of the promised help from Burgundy being forthcoming, Edward was happy to negotiate a ransom from his cousin of France.

Following detailed negotiations, in which the clever Morton was much involved, the Treaty of Pecquiny was signed on August 29th, by which Edward received an immediate payment of 72,000 crowns, an annual pension of 50,000 crowns for nine years, and the betrothal of the Dauphin Charles to his eldest daughter Elizabeth, then aged nine. Perhaps following the example of his Queen in her astute arrangements for the property of Cecily, her new daughter-in-law, it was further agreed that if Elizabeth should die before the marriage, then Charles would marry his second daughter, Mary who was a year younger than her sister. A final added bonus was that much of Edward's war-chest remained, still unspent, in England's royal Treasury.

Thus, Edward IV returned triumphantly and wealthy, if not victorious, to the bosom of his loving and approving family. Queen Elizabeth, who produced a fifth daughter, Anne, at the beginning of November, was inordinately proud that her oldest girl would now, one day, follow her example by becoming a reigning Queen, and took to referring to the Princess Elizabeth as "her little Dauphiness", or so it was reported in France. Such gossip did little to improve Gallic feelings about the projected match, or the enormous pension which had to be found yearly to satisfy England's King. However, Louis gave no hint of dissatisfaction with the arrangement, nor about further reports on the magnificent processions and celebrations which followed Edward's return home and which were clearly financed, at least in part, by French gold. Patience ranked high in the list of virtues of the King of France.

In George of Clarence, unhappily, equanimity had never been a strong point of character and events in 1476 would combine to bring to a head the growing bitterness between the King's discontented younger brother and his hated rivals led by the Queen. The five years since Tewkesbury was won had not been a period of unalloyed happiness for the Duke of Clarence. His attempt to keep the whole Warwick inheritance in the right of his wife, Isabel, had been prevented - unjustly as he saw it - by the King who insisted that their brother Richard had every right to marry Warwick's younger daughter, Anne, and to share thereby in the great wealth left by the Earl. In the upshot, Richard had been content to have Middleham and some of the surrounding estates, leaving the bulk of the fortune with Clarence, but George, who had once been but a single step away from the throne of all England, still felt badly done by.

His unhappiness was exacerbated by the differing treatment he and his brother Richard had at the King's hands. Richard of Gloucester was clearly the favoured one, the trusted one, holding the peace of the Scottish Border, keeping the north safe for Edward. Clarence on the other hand had vast estates, and wealth, and little purpose in life. He knew that Richard had acquitted himself far better at Barnet and Tewkesbury than had he, but he felt he had been given no opportunity for distinction; he believed Edward mistrusted him still, and railed at the injustice of it. If he had not rallied to Edward's standard at Banbury, bringing 4,000 men to join him, might not the cause of the House of York have been lost forever and which of them then would have survived the debacle? Neither of his brothers and none of the Queen's kin, that was certain. Clarence nursed his discontent and his growing hatred of the Woodvilles into the cold of Winter, 1476, when the final blows came.

On December 21st, his wife Isabel, daughter of Warwick, died shortly after giving birth to a second son, who followed her into the grave a few weeks later. A fortnight afterwards came news from Burgundy that Charles the Bold, tempestuous son of Duke Philip the Good, had paid the final price for the stormy temper for which he was famed and had been killed on January 5th 1477, while besieging Nancy. The heir to this great dukedom was, in fact, an heiress, Mary, daughter of Charles by his first wife, and her step-mother Margaret wondered whether the two tragedies might not provide an opening for further strengthening of the bonds between the Duchy and England. She sent to her brothers, Clarence and the King, proposing that the new-made widower should remarry and that Mary should be his bride.

George of Clarence, any remaining grief for his former wife quickly put aside, leaped at this golden opportunity and went at once to discuss it with his brother. Unhappily for him, the news had also filtered through to the ever-watchful Woodvilles and Elizabeth had worked her wifely magic on the King. The result was that Edward firmly refused Clarence permission to press his suit with the Burgundian heiress, and the Duke's consequent anger reached incandescent levels when he learned that Elizabeth had proposed her brother Anthony, Earl Rivers, as a suitable alternative and had secretly written to the Dowager Duchess Margaret offering the backing of an English army, if she would support such an arrangement.

This was one disappointment too many for the Duke of Clarence, one insult too far. Hitherto, he had made little secret of his dislike for the Queen and her family, now he published abroad his total disdain for this brood of commoners. He went further, noting that his brother had married a widow which was not an established practice on the part of kings and, on these grounds, suggested that the marriage was not lawful and that the offspring from it could not inherit the throne. The arrival of a third son, George of Windsor, in the early Spring of 1477, who was named for his uncle as conciliatory gesture by the King, did nothing to stem the growing flow of the Duke's venom.

George of Clarence was now treading on very dangerous ground and went further still when, in April, he had one of his late wife's attendants, Ankarette Twynyho, summarily arrested on charges of having poisoned Isabel. She was taken at once to Warwick, where Clarence's word was law, and there, with John Thuresby who was accused of poisoning Isabel's infant son, was tried and hanged. The clear implication left to be drawn was that the family descended from Melusine, the serpent-witch, the poisoner, to wit: the Woodvilles, had worked their wickedness on the innocent wife and child of that fine upholder of truth and justice, George, Duke of Clarence, brother to the King.

Queen Elizabeth, now effective head of the Woodville family, had had her fill of George of Clarence. With Warwick, he had planned and brought about the deaths of her beloved father and younger brother, he had placed her in peril of her life on several occasions, he made no secret of his contempt for her "low-born ancestry" and had imperilled the succession of her son to the crown. Now he debased the memory of her dead mother and threatened her own position once more with groundless accusations of the involvement of Woodvilles in the poisoning of his wife and child. It was time for the problem of George, Duke of Clarence to be solved, finally.

The initial Woodville gambit became apparent three weeks after the execution of their alleged tools in Warwick. One, Thomas Blake of Oxford, a clerk in holy orders, was arrested for treason and sorcery and during his questioning named Thomas Burdett, a friend of the Duke of Clarence and John Stacey, Clarence's household chaplain as co-conspirators. The three were found guilty of treasonably imagining and compassing the King's death and were executed on May 19th. Strangely, Blake, the originator of the charges raised against Clarence's people, was pardoned, presumably for turning King's evidence. Whatever the reason, Blake went free.

Further infuriated by the killing of men close to him, Clarence, while the King and Queen were at Windsor, forced his way into the Council Chamber bringing with him Doctor John Goddard who read out the dying declarations of innocence by Stacey and Burdett. Goddard was not particularly well-chosen for this task, since he had publicly supported the right of Henry VI to the throne at Paul's Cross, in 1470, and Clarence's added comments on the low-birth of the Queen, her family's habit of practising sorcery against any and all who displeased them, and the probable involvement of his brother the King in such necromancy added criminal foolishness to the folly already perpetrated.

Events were immediately reported to the Queen, who lost no time in taking her complaint about this continued persecution of herself and her family to the King. Edward was growing increasingly wrathful about Clarence's apparently unending capacity for idiocy, but still felt loath to move against his brother. However, when further reports came, via the Woodville faction, of Clarence writing to friends telling them to be armed and ready at an hour's notice, and Louis of France - ever one to stir a boiling pot - sent "friendly warning" of rumours circulating that Clarence had wanted the marriage with Burgundy as a spring-board to the English throne, the King gave orders for his brother's arrest and, in late June, had him committed to the Tower for the safety of the Realm.

Six months later, on January 16th, the day after the King's younger son, Richard of York, was married to his cousin Anne Mowbray, heiress of the Duke of Norfolk, a special Parliament met to hear the King's accusations against the Duke of Clarence, which ended with Edward declaring his brother guilty of High Treason. On February 8th, a Court of Chivalry presided over by Henry Stafford, the young Duke of Buckingham, pronounced sentence of death on George Plantagenet and ten days later, the Speaker of the Commons appeared at the Bar of the Lords to request swift dispensation of justice. George, Duke of Clarence, died the same night by means which have never been adequately identified.

The Woodville quest for vengeance was complete and while the King preserved much of their inheritance - in his own care - for his orphaned nephew and niece, some crumbs from the table fell and rolled in the direction of the Queen's eldest son, Thomas Grey, Marquess of Dorset. In addition, her brother Earl Rivers received estates valued at £100 per year in satisfaction of a debt on account of a loan he had made long before to his sworn enemy, the very wealthy Duke of Clarence.

Anthony Woodville, 2nd Earl Rivers

(Engraving from mss original in Lambeth Palace)

CHAPTER THIRTEEN

"...the king... took to his bed about Easter time and on 9 April
gave up his spirit to his Maker at...Westminster... in 1483..."

[Crowland Chronicle]

With Clarence gone, Elizabeth Woodville was able to give her whole mind to the problem of her brother Anthony's unmarried status and in June 1478 appeared the first fruits of her latest efforts. James III, King of Scotland wrote to Edward proposing that his sister Margaret should marry Earl Rivers, the King's brother-in-law, and thus further the improvement in relations between the two kingdoms. Edward IV, urged on by his wife, was very willing that such a marriage should take place and plans for the event began to take firm shape, the only interruption to their development occurring late in the year, when the Queen produced a sixth daughter, Catherine.

The year 1479 did not start well for Edward and his Queen. In March their infant son George died of the plague, and matters went from bad to worse when the Scottish Princess Margaret, who was expected to arrive for her marriage to Earl Rivers in the late Summer of the year, failed to appear. The canny James III had been delighted to receive the approaches of Elizabeth Woodville and to play along with her, so long as this suited the purposes of his secret sponsor, Louis of France. Now, as the Spider King's complex scheming matured, it was time for Scotland to throw off the mask of friendship and revert to their favoured pursuit of raiding over the Border. It was clear that a suitable match for Anthony Woodville would have to be sought elsewhere, and all over again.

By the Spring of 1480, it also became clear that the reiving along the Border was not an isolated raid or two, here and there, but a new border war in the making. In May, Edward sent to his brother, Richard of Gloucester, at his Middleham base, authorising the recruitment of levies in the northern counties to defend the estates under attack. In August, however, a strong force led by the Earl of Angus crossed the Border and looted and burned Bamburgh before retreating back to Scotland. Richard felt compelled to make a retaliatory raid and this he did to such effect that the Scots made no further incursions for the rest of the year, but, their original depredations had given King Edward cause for collection of a further "benevolence" to finance a larger operation against Scotland in 1481.

The Duke of Gloucester's success was followed closely by a further cause for royal celebration when Elizabeth Woodville bore her seventh daughter and, as it transpired, her last child, on November 10th at the new Palace at Eltham. She was christened Bridget by the Bishop of Chichester, with great pomp and ceremonial, involving a torchlight procession in which the baby was carried by Margaret Beaufort, Countess of Richmond, and now Lady Stanley, effective head of the House of Lancaster and mother of Henry Tudor. Bridget's godparents were her Grandmother, Cecily Neville, Duchess of York, her oldest sister Princess Elizabeth, and the Bishop of Winchester.

By the Summer of 1481, it became apparent that any Scottish plans for a major invasion had been cancelled, which was fortunate since Edward's efforts to raise funding for defence of the Border had not been entirely successful. However with Gloucester guarding the Marches and the Scots continuing quiet, King Edward felt able to visit Oxford in late September to mark the recent installation of Lionel Woodville, the Queen's brother, as Chancellor of the University. Lionel met the royal pair at Magdalen College where he gave a welcoming oration, the first of several such on succeeding days, and in the evening of each there was the feasting and roistering which occupied so much of Edward's time and attention in his later years.

The following month, Edward, whose health was not good, managed to journey north to Nottingham where he met his brother Richard to discuss a further campaign against Scotland in the Spring of 1482. It was planned that Edward himself would lead the expedition which would be designed to give the Scots such a bloody nose that their depredations would be ended for years to come. Their discussions and plans completed, the King and his brother parted, Edward southwards to the milder climes around London and his brother north to continue his task of keeping the Border safe. As an early commencement of the coming campaign, he opened a siege of Berwick, the great Border fortress ceded to the Scots years before by Margaret of Anjou as payment for their support of the House of Lancaster.

The Winter of 1481/82 was a time of bitter cold and followed on a bad harvest which left much of England, and Europe indeed, on short commons. However, Richard of Gloucester pushed forward as best he could with his plans for the invasion of Scotland and awaited his brother's arrival to launch the operation. In the event, the King's health was such that he had not taken up his command by May and Gloucester had to lead the first foray himself, advancing unopposed into the Lowlands and burning Dumfries. He then withdrew and rode to Fotheringhay where he met his ailing brother and the Duke of Albany, younger brother of James III, whom Edward proposed to put forward as a claimant to the Scottish throne.

By July, Gloucester was back in the borders, taking the town of Berwick and then hasting northwards to Edinburgh, burning and destroying as he came. James assembled a strong force to meet Richard, but his nobles had no stomach for a fight and arrested their King, then sent to Gloucester for terms. By this time, Richard of Gloucester knew that the Scots would not accept Albany as their King and therefore contented himself with exacting punitory fines and with having taught the Scots a salutary lesson in the arts of war. The English army then withdrew to Berwick where the citadel surrendered on August 24th - after more than 20 years of Scottish rule, Berwick was returned to England and the news of Gloucester's success was greatly welcome to his infirm brother and King, Edward IV.

The year 1482 had not been a good one for England, nor for its King, nor for the Queen and her Woodville family. The death of Lady Anne Mowbray, child bride of Richard Duke of York, late in 1481 had deprived the Queen of a handsome income, since the properties of the Mowbray heiress had reverted automatically to the Viscount Berkeley whose mother was a Mowbray. Elizabeth Woodville would immediately commence schemes to recover the wealth which she had regarded as her own for the four years of the marriage, but this would take time and she had realised that time was no longer on her side - her husband, the fount of all her, and her family's, wealth and power was in seriously failing health, and she had few illusions about their familial strength once the King's support failed.

Then, in the first days of Spring, news had come from Flanders that Mary of Burgundy had died following a fall from her horse on March 27th. This brought a bitter reminder of Elizabeth's failure to capture such a magnificent prize for her family - the Duchess had married Maximilian, son of the Emperor, who now held Burgundy for his two small children, Philip and Margaret. Sensing his moment had finally arrived, Louis of France started his planned end-game which would re-absorb the Duchy and all its appanages into the Kingdom of France. Burgundy was quickly swallowed, followed by Artois, and the French armies moved towards the final stronghold of Flanders. The Flemings - shrewd businessmen all and partially, and secretly, bought by Louis - refused to accept Maximilian's authority and the Burghers of Ghent seized power and demanded negotiations with France to end hostilities.

During the fighting, Maximilian had appealed again and again to Edward for help, but the war with the Scots and the very large annual pension paid by Louis to Edward had proved insuperable obstacles to English involvement in another field just as Louis had known they would. And, as a bonus, the King of England's excesses of bed and board had bloated his once magnificently healthy body and clouded his keen, fighting brain. Never again would Edward of York bestride a battlefield and snatch victory from the jaws of defeat and death. His race was run. And so it was that, at Christmastide 1482, when news arrived of the signing of the Treaty of Arras on December 23rd between Louis and Maximilian, which, among its many clauses, provided that Burgundy would never again support English pretensions to the French throne and, more shocking still, agreed that the infant Margaret of Burgundy would replace Elizabeth of York as the bride of the Dauphin, the King of England was grieved almost unto death.

Recognising this, Elizabeth Woodville put her own deep chagrin at the insult to her "little Dauphiness" to one side and immediately started planning how best to ensure her position in England after her husband's death. It was clear that control of her eldest son, who would follow his father as Edward V, was critical to the success of any scheme and, as the New Year dawned she sat with her sons Thomas and Richard Grey and her brother Sir Edward Woodville in her magnificent private apartments at Eltham Palace to decide their plan of action.

On January 20th, Parliament was summoned - the first of 1483 and the last of Edward's reign - and amid the business it transacted was confirmation of an agreement between the royal family and the Berkeleys which restored the Mowbray inheritance to the Duke of York. During the young Richard's minority, the income would again be applied by the Queen to the Duke of York's education and welfare generally. Further, a marriage between Thomas Grey the younger, grandson of the Queen, and Anne, daughter and heiress of King Edward's late sister Anne, Duchess of Exeter, was formally approved.

The King had already made generous provision for his daughters, in a new Will bequeathing each of them 10,000 marks as a marriage portion, and chargeable to the revenues of the royal Duchy of Lancaster, and with the proviso that his girls should be governed and ruled in the question of their marriages by Edward's "dearest wife" and by his son the Prince of Wales "if God fortune him to come to age of discretion." There would be further rich pickings in the future for Elizabeth Woodville when the question of each daughter's wedding arose.

On February 2nd, the feast of Candlemas, Edward and his Queen made a last, magnificent public show when they processed from St Stephen's Chapel to Westminster Hall and, during the procession, the King knighted Richard Wood and William Catesby. The King's health continued to give grave concern and by the end of March he had taken to his bed at his Palace of Westminster. There, on April 9th, 1483, having summoned Thomas Grey, Marquess of Dorset and Lord William Hastings to be reconciled in his presence, died Edward IV, last, great Warrior-king of the English in his 41st year.

His Queen, Elizabeth Woodville, was not present at the end - it was not considered fitting for women, however exalted their rank, to be involved in such solemnity as the death of a King demanded. In any event, she was already busy with the first phase of her plan to keep her hold on the reins of power. The new Monarch, her son Edward V, must be brought at once from Ludlow to Westminster and riders were already standing by to ride post-haste to the Marches carrying her summons to Anthony Woodville, Earl Rivers. Once in London, the new King would be crowned within two weeks of his father's death, an unusually short period, but essential to remove the need for a Protector of the Realm - Richard of Gloucester obviously - to be appointed. A crowned King would rule in his own right, with the guidance of his Council of Regency, which would be led in this case, against all custom, by Elizabeth Woodville, Queen-dowager.

Meantime, the dead King's body lay in state in the Chapel of St Stephen within the Abbey until April 18th when it left for its final resting place at Windsor. There, two days later, in the magnificent Chapel of St George, which Edward himself had enriched, he was left to his final rest amid the prayers of the highest in the land, though his wife and her family were busy elsewhere on more important matters,

Richard III

(Society of Artiquaries of London)

CHAPTER FOURTEEN

"We are so important, that even without the king's uncle we can make and enforce these decisions."

[Mancini/Armstrong]

While her messengers headed north-west to Ludlow, Elizabeth Woodville and her eldest son, Thomas Grey, were urging on the royal Council the necessity to celebrate the Coronation of Edward V as quickly as possible so that the realm should not be left rudderless for any lengthy period. It would be most natural for the Queen to head the Council of Regency which would also be required and she would be assisted in her work by her brothers, Earl Rivers, who had been appointed the young King's Governor by her late husband, Lionel, Bishop of Salisbury, and Sir Edward Woodville - newly appointed Admiral of the Channel fleet - and by her sons Thomas and Richard Grey.

The Queen's view was opposed by Lord William Hastings who stressed the vital importance of securing the assent of the late King's surviving brother to any arrangements put in hand and asked when messengers had been sent north to Middleham to convey news of Edward's death. Thomas Grey responded in a supercilious manner that no such message had been sent, since the council assembled was of sufficient importance to decide on the Kingdom's future government. Hastings made his excuses and left the chamber and, within the hour, other messengers were spurring hard on the road to Yorkshire, bound for Middleham Castle and the Duke of Gloucester.

For the moment, however, control of the Council and thence of the Kingdom was vested in Thomas Grey, Marquess of Dorset, and effective leader of the Queen's party. The only opposition came from Hastings and a handful of his fellow barons and they could do little more than delay the development of a government dominated by the Woodvilles. The key to the outcome of the struggle between the contending factions lay in the timing of the appearance of the new King in his capital and that of the advent of his uncle, Richard of Gloucester. Whoever came first to London would win all. With some difficulty, Dorset succeeded in persuading Council that the

Coronation of Edward V should take place on May 4th and the Queen sent again to her brother, Earl Rivers, to hasten his movements and to ensure that her son arrived in London no later than May 1st, fretting the while that the key element in her scheme was presently controlled by the dreamer of the family.

Anthony Woodville, Lord Scales, had succeeded to his father's Earldom fourteen years earlier following King Edward's recovery of power after Warwick's initial success at Edgecot. A man of many parts - and many contradictions - he was a brilliant jouster in the tiltyard and a careful avoider of the risks of real fields of battle; a devout Christian wearing, it was said, a hair shirt under the richest of garments; a scholar, linguist and patron of William Caxton; a widely travelled man who had made the pilgrimage to St James's Shrine at Compostella and had discussed - and no more than that - with Pope Sixtus IV the possibility of making a crusade against the Infidel. The Earl Rivers was, in brief, a mass of contradictions who enjoyed the good things in life but had not the burning ambition to acquire them which most of his siblings had inherited from their royal mother.

Typically now, Rivers delayed departure of the royal train for London so that Edward V might attend a splendid ceremony his uncle had devised in honour of St George. A message was received from Richard of Gloucester, who had realised what was afoot and was hastening towards London, suggesting that the two trains should meet north of London and Rivers took time to send a courteously guarded reply. But finally, on April 24th, King and Earl set out from Ludlow leading a great train of wagons escorted by 2,000 men at arms and archers. Their course lay eastwards to Northampton which they reached four days later and turned south on the road to London and the anticipated Coronation which would also crown Elizabeth Woodville's schemes with brilliant success.

It had been Anthony Woodville's intention to rendezvous with the Duke of Gloucester at Northampton but when the royal train arrived, he found Lord Richard Grey impatiently awaiting his coming, with a further urgent message from the Queen pressing her brother to make all possible haste to London and to waste no time waiting for Richard of Gloucester. Compliantly, Rivers moved on a further 15 miles southwards to Stony Stratford and billeted his column there for the night, but having become aware that the Duke of Gloucester was now close behind, and had indeed arrived at Northampton, decided it would be politic to visit him and explain that he had missed the appointed meeting in order to leave room in Northampton for Richard's train.

It was an implausible excuse offered by an unworldly man and it would cost Anthony Woodville his head before midsummer.

Gloucester invited the Earl to stay and eat and spend the night at Northampton, where, shortly afterwards, they were joined by Henry Stafford, Duke of Buckingham and brother-in-law to Rivers, who had brought 500 men to help Richard of Gloucester escort the new King to London. Older than his two companions, Earl Rivers retired early and the two royal Dukes - Buckingham was directly descended from Edward III - both now aware of the complex scheming of the Woodvilles to seize power, agreed on a decisive counter move which they would implement with the morning light.

At daybreak, Rivers awoke to find his lodging surrounded by the Dukes' men who had disarmed his own retainers and prevented news of the coup being sent to Stony Stratford. The whole force then moved quickly south and found the King's train assembling preparatory to travelling onwards to St Albans, Barnet and London. Richard Grey and the King's long-time tutor, Sir Thomas Vaughan, were arrested and the men they had led from Ludlow, now leaderless, were instructed to return to their homes since Edward V would now be escorted to his capital city by his royal uncle, Richard of Gloucester. The two Dukes, their men and their prisoners then returned to Northampton where Grey and Vaughan were held separately from Rivers and messengers rode hard for London to advise Hastings and his party that Richard of Gloucester had custody of the new King and would bring him to Westminster as soon as he had assurance that all was well.

Richard Grey's retainers had earlier left for London, riding equally hard, to bring the news of devastating failure and ruined hopes to Elizabeth Woodville, her brothers, and Thomas Grey. Their "best-laid scheme" had gone disastrously "agley" and the conspirators would doubtless be called upon to pay a heavy reckoning. Yet again in her life, Elizabeth Woodville gathered her family and made for the Sanctuary of Westminster Abbey, this time taking the bulk of the royal Treasury with her.

While Woodvilles fled abroad or fretted in the Abbey, William, Lord Hastings, rejoiced at the success of his counter-plot. At a stroke, his hated rivals had been cast down, their schemes shattered, and his arch-enemy Elizabeth Woodville would not control the crown of England as she had planned. The Queen had never really liked Hastings. She felt he had usurped the post her brother most desired as Captain of Calais, which Edward had conferred on his old comrade in 1471, and he was the King's greatest friend and confidant, totally outside the Woodville circle of influence. He was, therefore, a wild card breaking the Woodvilles' exclusive circle of influence around the monarch and, the Queen knew, was often her husband's boon companion in bouts of drunkenness and lewd behaviour.

For his part, Hastings was fully aware of the Queen's dislike and knew he would have short shrift from any government controlled by her and her family. He was delighted and relieved in equal measure, therefore, that his counter-coup had worked so well. He lost no time in publishing details of what had occurred at Stony Stratford to the many Lords and Knights who were in London preparing for the Coronation ceremonies scheduled to take place in four days' time and then sent to Richard assuring him that the city was quiet and looking forward to seeing its new King. Richard replied that he would enter the capital with the King and Buckingham on May 4th which would give the loyal citizens a cause for celebration in place of the cancelled crowning.

And so it was that on Sunday the 4th of May, King Edward V rode into London at the invitation of the Lord Mayor and assembled City Fathers, flanked by the two Dukes, to thunderous cheers from the populace. The bells of churches and cathedrals were ringing, adding their peals to the welcome, and the noise of the continuing plaudits as the procession wound its way up the hill to St Paul's and to the Bishop's Palace where the King would lodge that night, must have reached southwards and westwards and penetrated the thick walls of Westminster Abbey to tell Elizabeth Woodville that her son had met with the warm reception she had planned for him, even though she and the rest of the family were unable to share in it.

Servants and physicians continued to bring the Queen news of events outside her Sanctuary in the days following. Richard had been named Protector by the Council and had moved quickly to restabilise the governance of the Kingdom. Amongst his earliest actions was a successful effort to remove the threat presented by Sir Edward Woodville and his fleet, which was lying at anchor in the Downs. Experienced sea-captains were sent to sail amongst Woodville's ships mid-way through May, publishing Richard's promise of full and free pardon to any who would return to their true loyalty to the crown and very soon, the Admiral was left with only two vessels and, with them, headed for the French coast and safety. In his own ship he carried his share of King Edward's treasure to ensure he would not spend his days in poverty

Then came news that her son had moved from the Bishop of London's Palace to the royal apartments in the Tower and his Coronation had been rescheduled for June 24th and a Parliament was summoned for the 25th to confirm the succession of the young Edward V. In the last two weeks of May, Elizabeth Woodville received a visit from Margaret Beaufort, Lady Stanley, who had become a close friend in recent years and had carried the youngest Princess of the Queen's family, Bridget, to her christening. Along with savoury foods and wines, Lady Stanley, also Countess of Richmond and mother to Henry Tudor, brought the Queen news which shocked her. It seemed that Thomas Stanley, through his membership of the Council, had got wind of a plot by the Protector to assume the crown and to deal sharply with the Woodville family, including the Queen dowager. However, the Queen should not despair - many members of the Council were against the plan and intended to prevent Gloucester's coup, but to succeed, any counterplot needed a strong, experienced leader who commanded universal respect and whose loyalty to her husband's heir was unquestionable. That man could only be William, Lord Hastings.

Throughout her life, a dominant quality in Elizabeth Woodville's character was her ability to adapt quickly to adverse changes in her circumstances. Hence, it took little persuasion on the part of Margaret Beaufort to get the Queen's agreement to a course of action, in which her old enemy must play a key role, aimed at resecuring possession of the boy King and, if possible, killing the Protector and his ally, Buckingham, in the process. She would at once send to friends in the north and on the south coast to raise strength to aid the projected rising, indeed her son Thomas Grey, Marquess of Dorset, had been secretly leaving Sanctuary in disguise and he could now make his escape permanent and hasten northwards to rouse Woodville supporters there and elsewhere.

Margaret Beaufort eagerly thanked the Queen and assured her that the Council members loyal to her son would not rest until they had sufficient strength to put an end to the ambitions of Richard of Gloucester. She also had a further proposal; she knew that the Queen, to the surprise of some, had a very friendly relationship with Jane Shore, sometime mistress to King Edward. Mistress Shore was now consorting with Lord Hastings and if she could assist with the persuasion of his Lordship, then their hopes would be set that much higher. The Queen well knew the power of pillow-talk, having herself used the stratagem successfully many times to advance her family's advantage through the King and agreed immediately that she would send messages to the lady in question.

Margaret Beaufort left the Queen with mutual assurances on speedy action in the common cause and said she would maintain regular communication through her physician whom she could send to tend the Queen's health without arousing suspicion. Then she returned to her house well satisfied with the way her plan had been received. There was, in fact, no plot on the part of the Protector to assume the crown, but she, her husband and the clever Bishop of Ely, John Morton, were developing a long-term design aimed at placing her son, Henry Tudor, on England's throne, and an essential first manoeuvre was to sunder the two main props of the House of York, Richard of Gloucester and William Hastings. The opening had been played successfully, the pieces would soon be in place to move towards the end-game, the Countess of Richmond was well satisfied with her progress thus far.

She would have been more content still had she been able to foresee the shape of events immediately in prospect, which would force the Protector into the course she had fictionalised for him and trigger a chain-reaction which, in so short a space as two years, would destroy the centuries-old rule of the House of Plantagenet for ever.

*Detail from contemporary sketch of
the Badge of William, Lord Hastings,
believed to incorporate Hastings' face.*

CHAPTER FIFTEEN

*"Thus fell Hastings, killed not by those enemies he had always
feared, but by a friend whom he had never doubted..."*

[Mancini/Armstrong]

Margaret Beaufort, Countess of Richmond and senior surviving member of the House of Lancaster, and her co-conspirators, her fourth husband, Thomas Lord Stanley, and John Morton, Bishop of Ely, had a willing and gullible dupe to forward their designs. Henry Stafford, second Duke of Buckingham, was, after Richard of Gloucester, the highest-born peer in the land; his paternal descent came directly from Thomas of Woodstock, youngest son of Edward III and his mother, Margaret, was daughter of Edmund Beaufort, Duke of Somerset, killed at First St Albans, as was her husband. Thus, the blood-royal flowed thickly through Buckingham's veins and, as a youth, he had been forced into what he felt was a degrading marriage with Katherine Woodville, sister to Queen Elizabeth, and had cordially hated the whole family from his wedding day onwards.

On Edward's death, Buckingham sensed that his opportunity for revenge had come at last and he rushed to join and support Richard of Gloucester, who was clearly the only substantial barrier to a seizure of power by his detested in-laws. Richard was grateful for Buckingham's support and gave him a place in his Council, which he filled with considerable enthusiasm, speaking weightily and lengthily on every subject that arose for discussion, much to the transparent distaste of Lord William Hastings, who resented the intrusion of "new men" into the highest council of the land. The obvious dislike between the two was subtly encouraged by two of their fellow-councillors, Lord Stanley and the Bishop of Ely, and they, with Margaret Beaufort, found occasion for private briefings of Buckingham on the plot, allegedly being developed by the Woodvilles and Hastings, to seize the reins of power from the Protector, which Henry Stafford, in turn, passed to Richard as the product of his own intelligence service.

In the same way, the two conspirators, with unwitting help from other veteran members, encouraged Hastings' dislike for the new man by, as fellow old-hands, joining him in deploring the trust clearly given by Gloucester to the Duke of Buckingham. Then, with the pot boiling merrily, they sat back to wait their opportunity to exploit the growing divergence between the two. It was not long in coming. On a pleasant evening, early in June, Buckingham came in haste to Stanley's house to tell his aunt that the Bishop of Bath and Wells, Robert Stillington, formerly Chancellor to Edward IV, had visited the Protector secretly and given him some stunning news. According to Stillington, Edward had made a pre-contract of marriage with Lady Eleanor Butler before taking Elizabeth Woodville to wife, making his union with her bigamous and the offspring thereof illegitimate. There was no way Edward V could succeed to the crown.

The following morning, there being no meeting of the Council, Lord Stanley and John Morton waited on Lord Hastings and told him what Buckingham had said. Hastings had been half-expecting something of the sort from the hints dropped by Jane Shore during their love-making, and it was now clear to him that Richard intended to usurp the throne. He agreed with his fellow-councillors that only an immediate counter-coup, with an effective and respected leader, could thwart Gloucester and his accomplice, that vexatious, jumped-up incomer, Buckingham and, assured of the covert support of Stanley and Morton, their adherents and, for what it was worth, that of the Woodvilles, he agreed that Gloucester and Buckingham should be seized and, if necessary, killed at the next meeting of Council. This he would arrange by replacing the usual guards with trusted men-at-arms from his own retinue; they would take the two Dukes with such force as was necessary and thus ensure the legitimate succession of Edward V, son of his old friend and master, under the safe protection and tutelage of that faithful old Yorkist war-horse, William Lord Hastings.

The basics of the plan were simple: Hastings would hold Richard in talk before the meeting-proper opened and would ask Morton if he could send for strawberries for him from his garden. This would give Morton a reasonable excuse for leaving the room so that he could ensure Hastings' guards were ready to carry out the arrest of the Protector and awaited their master's signal. He would convey this to Hastings, on rejoining the meeting, by saying he had sent for the strawberries. Delighted that, at last, he was able to take drastic action against Buckingham, Hastings bade his colleagues farewell and set about his arrangements. Meantime, the other two returned to Stanley's house, and advised Margaret Beaufort that the plan was ready. She sent a messenger to Buckingham that she had urgent intelligence for him and, when he arrived post-haste, told him of the assassination plot prepared by the traitor Hastings.

Beside himself with rage, Buckingham immediately rushed to advise Richard of the intended perfidy and while Gloucester found it difficult to believe that an old comrade would go to such lengths as to plan his death, or that Hastings could combine happily with the Woodvilles, he accepted that it would be foolish not to take appropriate precautions. He would ensure that the guards at the next meeting were his own men and then wait to see if Hastings would condemn himself out of his own mouth by using the strawberries signal. If he did, then woe betide him. After Buckingham left, Richard spent much time writing and then summoned Richard Ratcliffe, his most trusted aide, and gave him messages to the Mayor and Council of York, and to other supporters in the north, asking them to send him armed support as quickly as possible. In the morning following, he had agreed with Buckingham, he would tell his secretary to send out a call for a meeting of the Council to be held on Friday, June 13th, in the White Tower at ten o clock. The time for action had come again.

When the councillors assembled on the day appointed, Hastings noted that they were a smaller group than was usual and Gloucester explained that their colleagues were meeting separately to finalise the details of the Coronation ceremony. As the others - Archbishop Rotherham, Stanley, Morton, Catesby - settled in their places Hastings asked Morton whether he had strawberries to spare and the Bishop said he would send for some immediately. He returned to his place saying all was arranged as requested and Richard of Gloucester rose to open the discussion. He had originally called the meeting, he said, to advise Council members of startling new developments affecting the succession, but first he must deal with another problem, involving a plot threatening the very lives of himself and his friends. How, he asked, should he deal with those planning to kill him, to which the Council gave the only response possible, the traitors should themselves be killed.

By now furiously angry, Richard crashed his fist on the table and shouted for the guards, who rushed into the chamber amid shouts of "Treason" and on Buckingham's direction seized Lord Hastings and pushed the other councillors to the far end of the room. Stanley stumbled in the melee and cut his head on the edge of the table, but was ushered back with the others. Hastings, at first dumbstruck by the change in his expected scenario, recovered his voice and protested his innocence but Richard would have none of it. The noble lord was taken out, given a brief moment to shrive himself, and then beheaded on a makeshift block formed from baulks of timber being used by builders for repair work. Thus, ignominiously, ended the life of a man who had risen high in a King's counsels and reached the great offices of state through his loyalty and faithful service, but who finally misplaced his trust in men who wished him ill and paid the price for it, in full.

Afterwards, Richard of Gloucester remained in his seat at the head of the Council Table and considered the others who had been present, conferring with Buckingham as to what further action, if any, might be needed. On the Duke's advice, he sent Stanley home to get his head attended to and ordered him to wait in his house until he was sent for. Thomas Rotherham would be lodged in the Tower's apartments pending further review of his involvement, but John Morton, Bishop of Ely, would, at Buckingham's specific request, be taken to the Duke's castle at Brecknock and lodged there for the immediate future. Buckingham was sure he would need continuing advice from this masterly civil servant in his own new role as chief adviser to the Protector, shortly to be King.

Meanwhile, Lord Stanley had reached his house and recounted the morning's events to his wife while she dressed his cuts. Their plan had worked to perfection, though the effective exile of Morton to the Welsh Border was unexpected. However, Margaret Beaufort felt this problem could be overcome by using Bray, her steward, to convey messages to the Bishop, while ostensibly carrying letters to her nephew, Henry Stafford, Duke of Buckingham. She would see Stafford that evening to ensure that Richard harboured no residual suspicions about a Stanley involvement in Hastings' plot, and then she would write to her son, Henry Tudor, to tell him of the advantageous developments. Immediately though, she would send her physician to tell Elizabeth Woodville of the sad failure of their plot and to advise her to adopt a low profile for the time being, while awaiting better times.

CHAPTER SIXTEEN

*"...Bounden am I, And that greatly, To be content. Seeing
plainly Fortune doth wry All contrary From mine intent...."*
[Verse written by Anthony, Earl Rivers]

An improvement in her fortunes seemed an unlikely prospect to Elizabeth Woodville after Margaret Beaufort's physician had taken his leave. All her plans for a recovery of her former power lay in ruins, thanks to the precipitate action of that fool Hastings, and she could see no end to her effective banishment as a Sanctuary Woman. Worse was to come. Three days after Hastings' execution, the full Council met to hear the Protector's account of events and the conspiracy leading up to them in which the Woodville family and their adherents had been deeply involved. It became clear that, for the realm's safety, a decision must be taken without further delay on the future of Earl Rivers, Richard Grey and Thomas Vaughan and with none dissenting, it was agreed that the three should be executed for their part in the original conspiracy and as a deterrent to those of their party minded to make similar plans in the future.

It was further agreed that the Westminster sanctuary did not provide fitting quarters for the King's younger brother Richard, Duke of York, and that the two boys would be more safely and comfortably housed together in the royal apartments of the Tower. To this end, the Archbishop of Canterbury, Thomas Bourchier, with a number of Lords from the Council, went immediately to see the Queen in Sanctuary and persuaded her that it would be better for her sons if they had each other's companionship. Reluctant at first, she eventually yielded to their arguments and the young Prince was conducted out of the Abbey by the Archbishop and conveyed by him to join his brother at the Tower.

On the following Sunday, at Paul's Cross, Friar Ralph Shaa, brother to the Lord Mayor, delivered a sermon to a large assembly of citizens and nobles, taking as his text "Bastard slips shall not take root". His theme developed around the right of the House of Plantagenet of York to the throne and revealed the pre-contract between Edward IV and Lady Eleanor Butler, which rendered his marriage to Elizabeth Woodville invalid and made the offspring of their union illegitimate. The true heir to the throne was the Protector, Richard of Gloucester.

The following day, Anthony Woodville, Earl Rivers, imprisoned at Sheriff Hutton Castle since his arrest at the end of April, was told of the Council's decision on his fate and that he, with Grey and Vaughan would be taken to Pontefract for execution. He was given a brief space and writing materials to make his will and transferred immediately to Pontefract where he met again Lord Richard Grey and Sir Thomas Vaughan. Their reunion was brief and, on Wednesday, June 25th, they were beheaded in the presence of Henry Percy, Earl of Northumberland and Warden of the Eastern March and of Sir Richard Ratcliffe who had brought the royal warrant for the executions from Westminster.

As the three men went to the block, the Duke of Buckingham was addressing the Parliament which had been summoned originally to greet Edward V, their new King. Instead, they heard a re-rehearsal of Shaa's revelations at Paul's Cross and Buckingham's view that Richard of Gloucester should be petitioned to take on the responsibility of ruling England. There was no opposition to this course and the next day a great procession assembled outside Baynard's Castle, the London home of Cecily Neville, where Richard was lodged, and Buckingham acting as spokesman begged him to take the crown. This Richard, having already realised there was no alternative, agreed to do and was acclaimed by all present as Richard III, King of England and France, and Lord of Ireland. He then led the mighty throng through London to Westminster Hall where he assumed the King's Seat and took the royal oath.

When Elizabeth Woodville heard of the debarring of her two young sons from the succession and of the deaths of her son, Richard Grey and her oldest brother, her cup brimmed over. With her she had only her five young daughters and a handful of servants, her sisters were scattered through the country in Sussex and Kent, Shropshire and Wales, her surviving brothers in exile or in hiding, and her first-born son Thomas Grey, Marquess of Dorset, was a fugitive who would assuredly die for his part in the abortive coup were he to be caught. It seemed the very nadir of her life's fortunes, but the final depth was yet to be plumbed.

Richard Plantagenet, erstwhile Duke of Gloucester, was crowned as Richard III on Sunday, July 6th, 1483, his wife, Anne Neville, daughter of the Kingmaker, beside him. It was the most magnificent royal occasion in living memory with Henry Stafford, Duke of Buckingham, playing with verve and gusto the role of master of ceremonies. The celebrations continued for a week and then, after approving a list of Honours and Offices in which the Dukes of Buckingham and Norfolk and Lord Thomas Stanley figured largely, on July 20th, the new King and Queen set out on a tour of their Kingdom to show themselves to their people. Buckingham helped to finalise arrangements and then rode home to Brecknock Castle where his own affairs awaited resolution and his guest, John Morton, was eager to hear of the great distinctions conferred on his noble patron.

Through this period of rejoicing, of which some echoes reached into the Sanctuary above Westminster Abbey, Elizabeth Woodville and her immediate family sank deeper into despair and despondency. The only small consolations the former Queen had were the infrequent contacts from adherents across southern England, and from her son, Thomas Grey, all of whom were continuing to plan for the day when the Woodville cause might rise again from the ashes. However, with Richard now enthroned to the acclaim of the English peerage and the London crowds, and planning a triumphal tour of his Realm to see and be seen by his people, it seemed that the family's fortunes were forever shattered. She confided these fears during the visits she received from her old friend Margaret Beaufort, who did not intend to join the King's train for his grand tour and who, after the coronation formalities, revived an old proposal which gave Elizabeth Woodville some cause to hope again.

In the period immediately following the triumphant return of Edward IV in 1471, which saw the extinction of the House of Lancaster at Tewkesbury, Margaret Beaufort - then in high favour with Edward following the death of her third husband, Henry Stafford, of wounds received fighting with the Yorkist army at Barnet - had proposed a union of York and Lancaster through a marriage between Princess Elizabeth and her own son, Henry Tudor. King Edward had not favoured the idea, since Tudor's claims to the throne were minuscule and he had hopes of betrothing his daughter to the Dauphin in due course. However, Margaret Beaufort had always kept this scheme in the back of her mind and brought it out again now to discuss with Elizabeth Woodville.

Eager to grasp at any straw, the ex-Queen expressed great interest in the idea, but wondered how it might be achieved while King Richard kept his throne. Margaret Beaufort agreed, but suggested the match would be supported also by Louis of France, with all that implied for financial and material support of a rising aimed at dethroning the usurper. The two ladies spent some time in animated discussion and parted with promises that each would, without any delay, initiate the necessary opening moves with their respective supporters. Each lady also made a small - unspoken - reservation in her position: Elizabeth Woodville, while pleased that her daughter might one day follow her as Queen of England, would prefer Richard's successor to be her son, Edward V; Margaret Beaufort, the shrewder of the two, recognised that this would be the other's true goal and, with Woodville support assured, had already decided to write to John Morton to get his views on the prospects for her scheme.

The Bishop of Ely was enjoying life in Buckingham's stronghold at Brecknock. True, it was a social backwater, but he had his books and papers, and could still learn of - and, indeed, play a part in - the affairs of the great world outside through Reginald Bray's regular visits. When he had heard from Margaret Beaufort about her talks with Elizabeth Woodville, he gave her plan a great deal of thought and found much therein to recommend it. The concept of a Welsh saviour returning to the island of Britain to reclaim Lancaster's rights from a Yorkist usurper was fundamentally sound. Properly organised and financed, it could set Wales and the Southwest in a blaze and with Woodville support across the southern counties and up into parts of the north as well, a rising could indeed be sufficiently widespread to have a fair chance of success.

However, he could see a major complication. Had Lady Stanley considered that a marriage with Elizabeth of York to reinforce her son's claim to the throne must, presumably, involve the re-legitimisation of the bride? And the fact that this would, automatically, restore the rights of her two brothers to the succession, which were superior to those of the Princess. To assure the success of her plan therefore, some drastic action might be required, which he felt confident could be inspired through the Duke of Buckingham - and his subtle brain saw still further possible uses for Henry Stafford in the event of his success with the first task - but he would like to have the views of Lady Margaret before proceeding and hoped she would let him have these without too much delay, since what had to be done, must be done quickly.

He now had her response - Bray had ridden hard and fast these past days and Morton had noted his dedication to his employers - a useful trait which might be applied elsewhere in due time - and smiled as he read. Margaret Beaufort's thoughts were as his own and she would rely on him to point Buckingham in the right direction. Her quick reply was most useful, since the noble Duke was expected at Brecknock within the next two days, which gave Morton enough time to think through his priming of Henry Stafford's mind and apply it immediately after he had arrived. No doubt Buckingham would be full of himself and his new status, his achievements and the new opportunities opening up before him thanks to his high-birth, his energy and to the advice he had received from John Morton. Yes, the Duke's mind would be very receptive to the ideas Morton wished to plant, which boded ill for the two young Princes in the Tower.

Arms and signature of Reginald (Reynald) Bray KG.

Henry Stafford.
2nd Duke of Buckingham

(Engraving taken from a traditional portrait)

CHAPTER SEVENTEEN

"...Ah, my poor princes ! ah, my tender babes !
My unblown flowers, new-appearing sweets....."
[Richard III]

Buckingham arrived early at Brecknock and could not wait to tell John Morton of his achievements and the honours the King had heaped upon him. He was now a member of the Royal Council, Great Chamberlain, High Constable of England, and would soon recover his family's title to the de Bohun lands which Edward IV had barred him from. Now it was clear to all that Buckingham was second in the Kingdom only to Richard himself. Now he could relax and refresh himself - he had spent little time resting through the long ride home - and hear his good friend and adviser's thoughts on the new sun which had risen on the fortunes of the House of Stafford.

Morton was lavish in his praise. The Duke had most certainly restored his family's fortunes and it was entirely right and proper that he should be given a place in the Kingdom appropriate to one who was a direct descendant of Edward III. The Bishop of Ely wished him well and would pray that nothing untoward should arise to mar this great success. It was the tone in which this pious hope was expressed which immediately caused Buckingham to pause in his process of self-appreciation - what exactly did his friend mean, what had he heard, how could there be any likelihood of his present glory being turned to ashes?

John Morton protested that Buckingham had inferred too much from his words, it was merely that he had reports from reliable sources within the Woodville camp that a new rising against the King was planned, aimed at re-seating Edward V on his throne. And, in the unlikely event that this effort should succeed, clearly King Richard would not survive, nor would any of those closest to him. Buckingham, ever volatile, changed in an instant from vainglory to rage. It was intolerable that this low-born family should constantly strive to raise themselves above their betters. They had caused the country enormous problems for nearly 20 years, loss of life, loss of treasure, loss - indeed - of honour, as who should know better than himself. It was time their plotting was stopped, finally. But what to do, how best to proceed? What would the good Bishop advise?

Morton protested weakly that his information might be wrong, perhaps all would still be well. If matters were left to develop further perhaps the whole plot would collapse for lack of real support. All of which merely confirmed Buckingham in his determination to take effective and decisive action immediately - he required a recommendation from his learned adviser on the best course to follow. Very well, Morton would suggest that the nub of the problem lay in the Tower - to which Buckingham as High Constable had full access. If the two boys currently resident there were, in some way, disposed of, then the problem would disappear - permanently. Not a fighting man in England would risk his life for the Woodvilles alone; their only leverage lay with the two royal bastards, descendants after all of Edward IV. Eliminate the boys and the problem would be solved.

John Morton was sure that the King would never find it in his heart to order the killing of his brother's children. But it was expedient for the security of the realm, the King's reign and the continuing success of all those close to the throne, that they should be removed. Presented with a fait accompli, Richard would recognise this and give appropriate reward and honour to any friend who might save his crown by recognising the threat which the two boys represented and having the courage to erase it. Buckingham was convinced. He would be the friend Morton had described and would take the decisive action required. Then he would ride after the King's train and tell him that his throne was secure, the land was safe from the Woodvilles, their bastard offspring were no more. And Richard's gratitude would indeed be boundless.

His strength renewed, Henry Stafford shouted for horses and men to be ready for an immediate return to London, and with barely another word to Morton he ran from the room, clattered down the stairs, galloped out of the castleyard, his escort struggling to stay with him. Impatiently he turned and shouted, calling on them to hurry, hurry. The High Constable of England had urgent business in London.

At the end of the month, the hard-riding Duke of Buckingham galloped through the gates of Gloucester and up to the castle bailey. Here the King's train rested prior to celebration of the royal arrival in the evening, and the weary, mud-spattered Henry Stafford, throwing off his fatigue, demanded instant private audience with Richard on a subject of overwhelming importance. As soon as Richard heard this he came to greet Buckingham and took him into a privy chamber, where his highly-strung, overwrought cousin told him of the Woodvilles' plot to dethrone him and replace him by restoring young Edward V. How he, Buckingham, learning of this dastardly scheme had gone at once to London and taken decisive action to prevent a rising now, or at any future time, against the King's lawful majesty. Using the authority given to him by the King as High Constable of England, and after swearing all involved to total secrecy on pain of instant death, he had removed this threat permanently - the two Woodville bastards were no more.

Horrified, stunned, hardly able to credit what Buckingham was telling him, King Richard's wrath was immense. He berated Buckingham as fool, murderer, madman and turned to summon guards - but stopped. As Henry Stafford had just said, the King had given him authority second only to his own. It was he, Richard, who had made it possible for this demented man to have access to Edward's sons. Who would believe that he had not also inspired, nay ordered, Buckingham to do what he had done. Meanwhile, the Duke - another Plantagenet - and with nerves fretted by his almost superhuman exertions of the past days, had not taken his verbal-thrashing in silence. The King's ingratitude was disgraceful, appalling. Where would he have been without Buckingham's support these past months? Who had countered the Woodville coup after Edward's death? Who had revealed Hastings' treachery and who had led Parliament to call on Richard to take the throne? He owed everything to Buckingham. Where was his gratitude?

Richard - icily still now - listened to his ranting and then bade him be silent. He knew he must continue with his progress, it was essential to the establishment of his reign. There was no time now to deal properly with Buckingham's awful crime, but he must be removed from the levers of power. He therefore ordered him to return to Brecknock and there to await a summons, when they would discuss these matters in detail. Meantime, the Duke would tell nobody else of what he had done, on pain of instant and dire retribution.

Buckingham, exhausted reaction setting in, realising at last the enormity of what he had done and how much worse he had made matters by his outburst, agreed and left the King and the castle to make his weary way westward to Brecknock and home. The two men never met again.

John Morton, Bishop of Ely, was clearly shocked by Buckingham's account of Richard's reaction to his method of terminating the threat from the Woodville bastards. He agreed with his patron, such ingratitude made any man unworthy of continued loyalty, indeed it would be prudent if the Duke were to take steps to protect his new power and his very life. The King had shown a ruthless streak in dealing with Hastings and it seemed highly probable that he would deal similarly with Buckingham once he returned to London. They must think and plan to pre-empt any hostile move by Richard and Morton had definite thoughts on an option which might be open to Buckingham. He would muse on it more overnight and they would talk again in the morning after the Duke had rested his weary frame.

Next day, Buckingham felt much recovered - he had the volatile Plantagenet temperament in full measure - and was eager to hear what Morton planned. The Bishop said that the rift with the King gave greater chance of success to an enterprise he had heard of earlier. It seemed Queen Elizabeth and Margaret Beaufort had discussed a possible rising by the remnants of Lancaster and the Woodville clique and were currently seeking help from Louis of France to bring Henry Tudor back to England at the head of an army which would join with and lead the rebels. This would obviously make for a strong force, capable of defeating Richard in the field, and now, if the strength which Buckingham could raise from Wales and the Marches were added, surely their combined might would provide an overwhelming army to unseat the usurper.

Richard's demise would, at a stroke, resolve Buckingham's problem. And he would gain much credit with Henry Tudor, the new King, who would assuredly be far more generous to the Duke than Richard had been. Henry Stafford was delighted at this swift change to his prospects and would start immediately on preparations through his loyal retainers. He would raise a mighty army and deal with the ungrateful King he had made, in the way he deserved. But, as he rose to leave Morton, the Bishop stayed his departure. There was now, of course, one minor snag to the projected alliance with the Woodvilles in the disappearance of the boys. If Queen Elizabeth were to hear of this then the whole enterprise might fall apart before it had properly begun.

Buckingham saw the point immediately and his mood swung again to despair, but, as always it seemed, the Bishop of Ely could provide an answer. It was fortunate that there was no regularity in the Queen-dowager's exchanges with her sons, the only communication was by intermittent assurances of their continued well-being, passed through friendly visitors and Lady Stanley could see to it that these were maintained. The King would have ensured that no word of the event got out, since he would certainly wish to tell the Queen-dowager what had happened himself, rather than sending word through an intermediary. So, the problem could be handled safely, and by the time Elizabeth Woodville learned that her sons were dead, Henry Tudor would be sitting on the throne of England and his chief adviser, his right-hand man, would be Henry Stafford, Duke of Buckingham, who need care nothing for what Woodvilles might think or say.

The spirits of the aforesaid nobleman, first peer in the Kingdom, rose once more. The Bishop, his good friend and counsellor, could always find a way through his difficulties, what a marvellous duo they made, what influence they would wield together as co-founders of the new dynasty. In high good humour, the Duke hurried from the room, he had many messages to send. John Morton smiled to himself and crossed to his own writing table; he had urgent news for Margaret Beaufort.

Signature and motto of Henry Stafford, Duke of Buckingham. He signs as "Harre Bokyngham", his motto: Souvente me souvene –"Remember me often".

Margaret Beaufort, Countess of Richmond.

(From a Portrait in St John's College, Cambridge)

CHAPTER EIGHTEEN

"...The Countess began to hope well of her son's fortune, supposing the deed would prove for the profit of the Commonwealth..."

[Polydore Vergil]

Margaret Beaufort, Countess of Richmond, read Morton's letter through and through again, then tore it into strips and threw the remains into the fireplace. She wrote immediately to her son, Henry Tudor, as the Bishop had suggested and then went to the Abbey Sanctuary with the good news of Buckingham's conversion. Elizabeth Woodville was delighted to hear of their powerful new ally and agreed it was essential for the three-pronged effort to be co-ordinated and that Margaret Beaufort was best-placed to ensure this happened. The Queen dowager would pass word to her son, Dorset, to warn their friends to be ready at any time after the harvest was in, but to wait for the final word from her before moving against the King.

Thomas Grey, Marquess of Dorset, had been in hiding in Yorkshire since leaving sanctuary, moving amongst the Woodvilles' friends there, constantly urging the necessity to keep the cause of Edward V alive. When he heard from his mother of the new hope for their cause - news closely followed by reports of the death of Louis XI on August 30th - he moved south to Wiltshire and there joined with his uncle Lionel, Bishop of Salisbury, in stirring trouble. Through the south-eastern counties, friends and relations of the Woodville family, under the leadership of Richard Guildford, son of a close friend of the late Earl Rivers, were banding together secretly, waiting for the call to rise against King Richard, And, in the southwest, Sir Thomas St Leger, who hoped to betroth his daughter to Dorset's son, was active in the Woodville cause and soon was linking with the Courtenays and other Lancastrian faithful rousing to the call of Margaret Beaufort.

By mid September, a widely-based conspiracy had come into existence, and further fuel was added to drive this intrigue forward when Margaret Beaufort, judging her moment to perfection, broke the news to its leaders that Richard's greatest ally, Henry Stafford, Duke of Buckingham, would lead a great army of Welshmen and Marchers to join the common cause. This raised expectation to a fever pitch and it was clear that a date must be set for the action to begin; the final piece in the mosaic - the advent of Tudor with his army of Bretons - must be put in place without further delay. And, at the end of the month, the news arrived, Henry Tudor with a mighty fleet and 5,000 men-at-arms at his back would sail for England to claim his throne in days rather than weeks. The word went out from the Countess of Richmond, the country would rise as one on October 18th, 1483.

Unhappily, for all the careful preparation and scheming put into the plot by the two great ladies, they had not allowed for the traditional delight in raiding London, endemic among Kentish men since the days of Jack Cade and, no sooner had firm word of the rising reached them than the county, aflame with excitement, was "up" and preparing to march on the capital. This news reached John Howard, Duke of Norfolk, and the King's Council in London some ten days before the time appointed for the rising and Norfolk raised men and marched out of the city to confront the rebels, his main objective being to prevent their crossing the Thames. At the same time, he sent word to Richard of the actions he was taking and added the even-more disturbing news that the Kentish men were proclaiming Buckingham as leader of the revolt.

King Richard received news of the rebellion and Buckingham's betrayal at Lincoln as he was making his way southwards to London towards the end of his Grand Tour. He immediately moved to Leicester, summoning all loyal Lords and men to join him there and by the last week in October having assembled a force several thousands strong, he moved towards Coventry with the intention of meeting Buckingham and his army advancing from the Welsh Border and cutting off the head of the revolt. The Woodville-inspired rising in the southeast was pinned south of the Thames by Norfolk and reports from the southwest indicated that the Lancastrian sympathisers there were waiting on events elsewhere. If Buckingham and his men could be destroyed, the rising would be effectively over.

In the event, the rising had fizzled out in torrential rainstorms which swept western England in the latter half of October. Buckingham's army, ill-prepared, smaller than he had hoped and continually harassed by attacks from bands of loyalists had, almost literally, dissolved and the Duke, deserted by his erstwhile adviser, John Morton, had fled into hiding. When he heard this news, the King turned his own army southwards to deal with any hardy rebels in the southwest of his realm, reaching Salisbury at the end of October without meeting any resistance. Here, the Duke of Buckingham was brought in, still dressed in his disguising rags, having been betrayed by a former servant whom he had trusted to conceal him, and Henry Stafford received summary justice for all his crimes on November 2nd, when he was beheaded in the market square.

A few days later, the promised fleet from Brittany arrived off the south coast bearing Henry Tudor and little else. The original armada of 15 vessels had been scattered and driven back to France by Channel gales and only Henry's ship and a single consort appeared off Poole in Dorset and then meandered west to Plymouth, where, despairing of finding the triumphant rebel host they were seeking, they turned away to return to Brittany. The grand rebellion had lasted less than a month, the Woodvilles and their supporters were dead or fled, Margaret Beaufort's leading role in the revolt was known to the King, and John Morton was on his secret way to exile in Flanders, via hiding places in the fens surrounding his diocese of Ely. The position of Elizabeth Woodville and her daughters was parlous in the extreme.

During the last two months of 1483, King Richard dedicated most of his time to making peace with Brittany and to resettling the south and southwest of the country. Early in January, he set off on a new royal progress through Kent and firmly re-established his authority in the county by appointing men loyal to himself to the key offices in the main towns. On the 23rd of the month he was back in Westminster for the opening of a Parliament which had originally been summoned for November but was postponed due to the rebellion.

Elected as Speaker was one William Catesby, formerly chief secretary to William, Lord Hastings, and now a fast-rising star in Richard's following. The Parliament passed Bills of Attainder against the chief rebels and formally enacted the settlement of the crown upon the King and his heirs through Titulus Regius. Among those adjudged guilty of treason or of supporting the rebellion were Margaret Beaufort and Elizabeth Woodville. The Countess of Richmond was not formally attainted following an arrangement by her husband, Lord Stanley, with the King, whereby her titles were forfeited and her lands passed into Stanley's safe-keeping as due reward for his overt loyalty during the rebellion.

Elizabeth Woodville, Queen-dowager, was similarly deprived of all her property, but the worst effects of this formality were mitigated through secret negotiations between her and the King which were being actively pursued while Parliament was still sitting. During these discussions, Richard revealed to his sister-in-law the awful fate which had overtaken her sons at Buckingham's hands and, after her initial shock and hysteria was past, had been able to demonstrate his own innocence of ordering, or perpetrating, any harm to the boys. She had seen and heard sworn statements from Sir Robert Brackenbury, the Tower's Constable - widely respected as a just and honourable knight - and his guards that the crime had been carried through in total secrecy by the Duke of Buckingham and his men alone, and that the few, indirect witnesses involved had been sworn to perpetual silence on pain of death.

The outcome of these discussions was an event unique in English History. On March 1st, 1484, nine days after Parliament had ended its deliberations, King Richard appeared at Westminster in a public ceremony before an assembly of Lords and Bishops with the Lord Mayor of London and his Aldermen to swear that, if the five daughters of Elizabeth Woodville and his brother Edward came out of sanctuary, he would do them no harm, he would care for them and their future welfare and provide marriage dowers for each of them to a yearly value of 200 marks. In addition, Richard swore to provide an annual stipend of 700 marks for the support of "Dame Elizabeth Grey" during her lifetime.

The self-imposed confinement of Elizabeth Woodville and her daughters was at an end and they emerged again into normal life. Further, the former queen had received private assurances from Richard that her surviving son, Thomas Grey, Marquess of Dorset, would be dealt with mercifully should he wish to return to England. She would write to him in Brittany and tell him of the King's clemency, urging his return to court, but this would be prevented by the French who, when they learned of the raprochement, saw no advantage in aiding the new King of England to heal further the political scars which marred his reign.

Margaret Beaufort - now, by her husband's favour - in her castle at Deeping, and John Morton, penniless Bishop of Ely exiled to Flanders, had no comforts offered to remedy their discontentment. For them, the only solution was that Henry Tudor should assume the crown of England and, while they could look for no further help from the Woodvilles to that end, they would continue planning and working towards that day. What else was left for them to do?

Sir William Catesby.

(From a memorial brass in Ashby St Legers)

CHAPTER NINETEEN

"The King...in the presence of the Mayor and Citizens of London, made the said denial in a loud and clear voice..."
[Crowland Continuation]

Richard III was well aware of the plots and plans being made in Brittany, France and Burgundy against his reign and saw, by the middle of the Summer of 1484, that the scheming was moving progressively towards support for the doubtful claims of Henry Tudor to the crown of England. On Christmas Day of 1483, following his escape after the disastrous rising against Richard, Tudor had formally vowed in the cathedral at Rennes that he would return to England, take the crown and marry Elizabeth, oldest child of Edward IV, thereby reuniting the sundered royal Houses of York and Lancaster. All the intelligence since received by Richard made clear that support through men and money and arms would be given to Tudor by his enemies on the Continent; it was no longer a question of 'if' but rather of 'when' this would happen.

The King had therefore based himself in the great keep of Nottingham Castle, whence he could move easily and quickly to any part of his realm, for, though he knew that Tudor would indeed come - and soon - he did not know where the landing would be made. Meantime, the Scots, encouraged by French gold, were again threatening the Borders and indulging in piratical raids by sea, requiring urgent and severe counteraction, which was forthcoming in such measure that James III sued for a permanent peace treaty. This was duly signed in Nottingham Castle at the end of September, 1484, with the two countries agreeing to a three-year truce, to be sealed by a marriage between Anne, daughter of Richard's sister, the Duchess of Suffolk, and James, Duke of Rothesay, heir to the Scottish throne.

There was, unfortunately, a corollary to this success, in that the opportunities for French mischief to be stirring in England were now limited to the single possibility of invasion by Henry Tudor, and the designs of the French Council of Regency, effectively led by the Dukes of Orleans and Bourbon, were centring exclusively on a descent, probably on the Welsh coast and certainly no later than the Summer of 1485. Under this threat, King

Richard's court prepared for the Christmas feast which would end a year already deeply shadowed by the death of Richard and Anne's only child, the young Prince of Wales in the early Spring - and in which the capacity for tragedy was not yet spent.

The King kept Christmas at Westminster and great efforts were made to make the festivities particularly magnificent and enjoyable. On the one hand it was important that foreign watchers should see England's King hale and hearty, among Lords and subjects who loved him well and rejoiced with him in the renewal traditionally deriving from the anniversary of Christ's birth. On the other, Richard's Queen was seriously ill; like her sister Isabel, Duchess of Clarence, who had expired at twenty four years of age, Anne had always been delicate of frame and the death of her only child weighed her heavily with grief. This, it seemed, might well be her last Christmas and it was important therefore to make it as happy as it could be.

An important factor in the gaiety engendered by the festivities was the role taken by Richard's nieces, the daughters of Edward IV, who, freed from their prisoning in the Abbey Sanctuary, were particularly blithe, rejoicing in their new-found freedom and the finery of their new gowns. Whatever relief the Yule-tide revelling brought to the Queen, formerly Anne Neville, younger daughter of Warwick the Kingmaker, its effect was short-lived and on March 16th following, while London was darkened by an eclipse of the sun, she died. The King was distraught, his cup of sorrow brimmed over, but still more was to come.

In her modest country house, Elizabeth Woodville kept in touch as best she could with events at court and had recovered much of her former spirit. However, the allowance made for her upkeep by the King was as nothing compared with her former riches as Queen of England and she thought constantly about ways of recovering some, if not all, of her former grandeur. When the news arrived of the Queen's terminal sickness, Elizabeth Woodville mused on the opportunities which could open before her, with the imminent death of Anne Neville. Richard had no heir, he would need to marry again, and where would he find a better wife than her own Elizabeth? Papal dispensation would be needed, but that could be secured through judicious disbursements in the right quarters. Yes, it was a brilliant concept and she would, immediately, take delicate soundings with people of influence, with members of the Great Council, and, eventually, with the King himself. She hurried to her writing desk.

The fruits of Elizabeth Woodville's probings were quickly apparent in the spate of rumours which arose that Richard intended to marry his niece and had, indeed, probably murdered his wife to facilitate a union with a younger, sturdier and, almost certainly, more fertile woman. The King's reaction was angry, such lying tales were beneath contempt and to be ignored, but his chief advisers, among whom William Catesby and Richard Ratcliffe were particularly aware of the effect such gossip was having on public opinion in the capital, pressed him to make a formal denial. Reluctantly, Richard accepted the force of their argument and at Easter tide, which fell in early April, he summoned the Lord Mayor and citizens of London to a public gathering at Clerkenwell and gave the lie, unequivocally, to the rumours which were circulating to his and his niece's discredit. He would hear no more of such vilification and so that there should be no further reason for this slander, he would send his niece to join her cousin, Edward, Earl of Warwick, who was lodged in the fresher, cleaner surroundings of the family castle at Sheriff Hutton.

Elizabeth Woodville, another of her schemes ending in disaster, felt it wisest not to broach her idea with the King. Clearly, if she were ever to resume her former dignity and wealth, it could not be through an incestuous union between her daughter and her royal brother-in-law. Like Margaret Beaufort and Lord Thomas Stanley, she would wait on events. One day, she was sure, her star would rise again - she had only to wait.

Another noble lady, Margaret Beaufort, quondam Countess of Richmond, was taking more active measures to ensure her future role in the governance of England. Through the tireless efforts of the hard-riding, totally-loyal Reginald Bray, she maintained a regular clandestine correspondence with her son, Henry Tudor, in his French exile and, as the Summer approached, it was becoming increasingly clear that his hosts were pressing him to make another bid to seize the English throne. Richard could not be allowed to establish his rule, since this would free him to tackle unfinished business elsewhere and the French Regent and her Council were not enamoured of the idea of another Plantagenet reviving his familial claim to the throne of France.

Towards the end of July 1485, a weary Reginald Bray galloped through the gates of Deeping Castle with an urgent letter for his mistress. Henry Tudor had sent his final letter from France. On the first day of August her son would sail from Harfleur with John de Vere, Earl of Oxford, who had nearly won the day for Lancaster 14 years before at Barnet and would now lead Tudor's army. With him also would be his uncle, Jasper Tudor, formerly Earl of Pembroke, a motley assortment of English exiles including Sir Edward Woodville and some 2,000 French and Bretons who had earned their release from jails by agreeing to accompany Henry Tudor on his desperate venture.

This, Tudor urged, would be his one and only chance to recover England's throne. Now was the time for his mother to aid him with money, reinforcements, arms and munitions, and, above all, the allegiance of her husband Lord Thomas Stanley and all his retainers to the cause of Lancaster. Margaret Beaufort knew her son was right, the moment had come. This time it would be death or dominion, there would be no mercy for the vanquished. She had more letters to write and the indefatigable Bray must take them to the Beaufort adherents in the west country, but first he should go to Nottingham and tell Lord Stanley, Constable of England, that his wife needed urgently to talk with him. Indeed, she would speak with him on matters of life and death.

Henry Tudor landed in the bay of Milford Haven in the southwest corner of Wales on Sunday August 7th, 1485 immediately unfurling Cadwallader's Dragon Standard and falling on his knees to kiss the earth and pray for God's blessing on his cause. He advanced northwards and westwards, gathering men and supplies, writing to his mother and to Welsh chieftains urging his desperate need for money and men and then swinging eastwards at last and arriving at Shrewsbury on August 13th where funds from his mother reached him, together with the news that Sir William Stanley was moving from the family lands in Cheshire with a large force to his support, while his step-father, Thomas Stanley, lay between Newport and Stafford with further reinforcement.

Moving to Newport, Tudor was joined by Sir Gilbert Talbot, son-in-law to the late Lord Hastings and blood-kin to Lady Eleanor Butler who had been scorned by King Edward, to the gain of the Woodvilles. There was no love lost between the Talbots and the Plantagenets, in proof whereof, Sir Gilbert brought in 500 men to serve under Tudor's banner. The army moved on to Stafford, reaching the town on August 16th and there Henry Tudor met Sir William Stanley who advised him to march to Lichfield, pick up artillery pieces left there by Lord Stanley and then make his way via Tamworth towards Leicester where the usurper, Richard, was gathering his forces. Tudor took this advice and on August 21st his army was making camp for the night at a place called White Moors, three miles southwest of Market Bosworth, a small town in Leicestershire. The Earl of Oxford's scouts returned to report that King Richard's army was encamped a few miles to the east at a village called Sutton Cheyney and it was clear to all that the morning must bring a decisive confrontation between the two opposing forces.

Neither side knew, with total certainty, the intentions of Sir William and Lord Thomas Stanley, whose forces had taken position on either side of the axis between the two main armies. Richard still hoped that Thomas Stanley at least might join his force with his King's; Henry Tudor hoped that both would attack the Yorkist power in the flanks in support of his own assault, John de Vere was content that, at worst, the Stanleys would not support Richard, since this, he felt, would give him superiority in numbers. He was probably the only commander in the two hosts who passed a restful night.

Sheriff Hutton Castle from an Engraving by S & N Buck
(Geoffrey Wheeler)

122

CHAPTER TWENTY

"...We will unite the white rose and the red.
Smile heaven upon this fair conjunction..."
[Richard III]

On the morning of August 22nd, 1485, the rule of the House of Plantagenet, which had endured in England for three centuries, came to an end. Betrayed by Stanleys, abandoned by Percy, Earl of Northumberland, his army badly arrayed to cover too many contingencies, Richard III, King of England for little more than two years, plunged to defeat and death in a last wild charge, aimed at snuffing out his rival's challenge along with his life. Henry Tudor, already wearing the battle-crown which had fallen from his predecessor's casque, accepted the allegiance of his victorious commanders, joined now by the Stanleys, to whom, in his first grand geste, the new King gave the spoils of the field. Perhaps it seemed most fitting that the birds of prey should feed their fill on the carrion they had made.

And then, on to the important matters. First, word must go immediately to Margaret Beaufort, who should join her son as soon as he came to his capital. Likewise to John Morton in Flanders, his royal master would have great need of the shrewd counsel of both these mentors now. Further, there was the question of his Christmas vow to marry Elizabeth of York as soon as he achieved secure rule in England. This could wait for a little while yet, but the girl should be brought from Sheriff Hutton castle to London and lodged there with her mother. Immediately, it was necessary for the new King to be crowned with full pomp and ceremony and, once that was done, he would have leisure to consider where and when his marriage should take place. His mother, he was sure, would bless the day her years-old plan had come to fruition and no doubt his mother-in-law to be would be equally happy at recovering much of her former status in the realm.

The Crowning to which Henry Tudor and his mother had looked forward for so many years was, initially, delayed by an outbreak of the sweating sickness in London, but on Sunday, October 30th, 1485, the Coronation of Henry VII finally took place at Westminster Abbey. Prior to the ceremony, the Coronation Honours List was published in which rewards were bestowed by the new monarch on those who had helped him to his throne, including his uncle, Jasper Tudor, who became Duke of Bedford and his step-father, Thomas Stanley, who received the Earldom of Derby. His first Parliament, summoned for November 7th, duly assembled and restored all property and estates to his mother, the new Countess of Derby, reversed all attainders against supporters of Lancaster and attainted all who had supported Richard III and confirmed that "the inheritance of the crown...be, rest, remain and abide" in the King and the heirs of his body.

Elizabeth Woodville's dignity as Queen-dowager and the legitimacy of her children was effectively restored by the repeal of Titulus Regius, unread, and all copies ordered to be destroyed. Finally, on December 10th, when the usual grant of tunnage and poundage for life was made to the King, his loyal representatives also took the opportunity to petition him to take Elizabeth of York to wife and he graciously answered that he was prepared to comply with their request. In addition, at the Queen-dowager's request, Henry summoned Thomas Grey, Marquis of Dorset, her eldest son, home from Paris where he had been left as hostage for the loan from the court of France which Henry Tudor had needed to mount his invasion. With the marriage date set for January 18th 1486 and her surviving family once more around her, Elizabeth Woodville could again take stock of her position and plan for the future with some assurance.

Towards the spring of the year, Henry Tudor was graciously pleased to grant various lordships to his wife's mother to be held by her during her lifetime. These were made up of half-a-dozen manors, which had been part of her dower after the death of Edward IV, and Letters Patent evidencing the grants were dated March 4th 1486. On the day following, Henry granted a small annuity to the Queen-dowager in "full satisfaction" of any claim she might have laid to the residue of her former estate.

On July 10th, Elizabeth Woodville took a lease on the Abbot's House at Westminster, which was a convenient location from which to visit her daughter when the court was resident in Westminster or Greenwich. The hoped-for coronation of the new Queen Elizabeth had, however, been postponed due to her majesty's pregnancy and, shortly after his mother-in-law's move into Westminster, the King returned from a progress around his northern shires and took his wife off to Winchester to await the arrival of their first-born. There in the ancient capital of Wessex, on September 20th, 1486, the Queen was delivered of a son who, on the following Sunday, was christened with Elizabeth Woodville standing as his Godmother and the Earls of Derby and Oxford as Godfathers. The infant prince was named Arthur and the Tudor dynasty was established.

The first year of Henry Tudor's reign had not been without incident and risings in Yorkshire and Cornwall had to be put down forcibly. In 1487, however, came news of a pretender to the throne, claiming to be Edward, Earl of Warwick, son of George of Clarence, who was raising the Yorkist standard in Ireland, backed by John de la Pole, Earl of Lincoln and formerly named as heir to the throne by his uncle, Richard III, with Francis, Viscount Lovell close friend of the late King, the Earl of Kildare, and other Lords and gentry. The pretender was crowned in Dublin as Edward VI on May 24th and landed on the Lancashire coast on June 4th, leading an army of 2,000 German mercenaries provided by the Dowager Duchess of Burgundy, Margaret of York, and backed by several thousand wild Irishmen.

King Henry had intelligence of the impending invasion through spies in the pay of his Chancellor, and newly-enthroned Archbishop of Canterbury, John Morton, and when news of the landing came he summoned all his power to rendezvous at Nottingham Castle. There, on June 14th he held a council of war with John de Vere, his chief general, Jasper Tudor, Duke of Bedford, who had brought his Welsh levies with him and Lord Strange, heir to Thomas Stanley, the King's step-father, who had with him 6,000 well-armed men to form the backbone of the royal army. The enemy force had already been located by de Vere's scouts some miles to the northeast and it was agreed that Henry's army should move to meet them, marching, unusually, in battle order. On the 16th of June the two armies met a mile south of the small Nottinghamshire village of East Stoke and, after some initial success for the Yorkist forces, their resistance was worn down by the better-armed, better-led royal army and they broke and fled.

The Germans died on the field, the Earl of Lincoln with them, and many of the Irish were killed in flight or drowned in the River Trent. Others were captured and taken to Lincoln where they were hanged on public gibbets as an example of what happened to rebels against the King's Tudor majesty. The so-called Edward of Warwick was captured and revealed as one Lambert Simnel, who bore an unfortunate resemblance to a possible heir to England's throne and was sent to work as a scullion in the King's kitchens. Francis Lovell again escaped the slaughter, but was never seen again - legend has it that he was found hiding in the cellars of his home, Minster Lovell, and was walled up there by order of his unforgiving King.

One other to feel the rancour of the insecure monarch was Elizabeth Woodville who had, inadvisedly, become involved by secretly urging her family's supporters to strengthen Simnel's cause. Her fault was uncovered by Margaret Beaufort, who had, in the course of an angry exchange with the Queen-dowager, let slip her own involvement in the deaths of Edward V and his brother, Richard, which had, predictably, led to so violent a swing in Elizabeth Woodville's allegiance. To protect his mother's reputation and the pious honour of his Chancellor and to remove a possible threat to the happiness of his marriage and a proximate, if feeble, hazard to his throne, Henry decided that Elizabeth Woodville must be placed in secure confinement. Accordingly, through his Council, it was decreed that because the Queen-dowager had delivered her daughters out of sanctuary into Richard's hands two years previously, she should be cloistered in the nunnery of Bermondsey and her lands and goods should be forfeit to the crown.

Elizabeth Woodville was to spend the rest of her life in Bermondsey, where, it is said, it was almost thought dangerous to visit her, or see her. She had brief cause for hope of better things, when Henry Tudor appeared to give "serious consideration" in the early months of 1488, to a proposal from James III of Scotland to marry her, which came to nothing when James was assassinated after being defeated at the battle of Sauchieburn in June of the same year. A month later, news arrived of the death of her brother, Sir Edward Woodville, who had pursued a career of knight-errantry on the Continent and, unusually among the men of his family, was slain in battle at St Aubin du Cormier, fighting for the Bretons against the French. A further short respite came when she joined her daughter, the Queen, in giving audience to her cousin by marriage, Francois de Bourbon, Comte de Vendome and husband of Marie of Luxembourg, in November 1489, at which Margaret Beaufort was also present.

Elizabeth's last surviving brother, Richard Woodville, third and last Earl Rivers, died in March 1491. Lttle more than a year later, Elizabeth Woodville, Queen-dowager of England, was stricken by a terminal illness and on April 10th dictated her last will and testament. This was a short bestowal, for which she apologised, stating that she had no worldly goods "to reward any of my children, according to my heart and mind" and the Executors were named as John Ingilby, Prior of the Charterhouse of Shene, and William

Sutton and Thomas Brente, Doctors. Two months later, on June 8th, the Friday before Whitsuntide, she died and was given the humble funeral which, according to report, she had requested. She had no moneys to cover large-scale funeral expenses, nor, it would seem, any close relative of sufficient means, or generosity, to furnish this deficiency.

She was interred on Whitsunday at Windsor, as she had requested, in the same tomb as her husband, Edward IV, at 11 o clock at night. There was no ringing of a funeral knell, no reception of the cortege by the Dean or Canons in their habits and no family representative among the five mourners present at the interment, other than Grace, a bastard daughter of Edward. There was no dirge and no solemn mass was sung. As she had requested in her will, her body was buried "without pomp entering or costly expenses done thereabout".

In the four days following, efforts were made to provide some of the "pomp" which Elizabeth Woodville had eschewed, with a requiem mass on June 13th and a sung mass of Our Lady on the day following. Among the dignitaries attending were the Queen-dowager's three younger daughters, Anne, Katherine and Bridget - the Queen herself was heavily pregnant - and Thomas Grey, Marquis of Dorset, each and all of whom made an offering of a single gold piece. Dorset then gave the customary dole, and after the ceremony paid, to "persons present", the comparatively modest sum of 40 shillings as reward for their costs.

Thus departed this life Elizabeth, Queen-dowager of England, first of the large, star-crossed brood of children born of the long-lasting love-match between Richard Woodville and Jacquetta of Luxembourg and last to die, excepting only her sister Katherine, once Duchess of Buckingham and, after re-marriage, wife to Jasper Tudor and, thereby, Duchess of Bedford. Katherine had also aspired greatly but was, perhaps, content with a little less than the stars and died early in the reign of her great-nephew Henry VIII, twenty years after the eldest and greatest of her siblings.

Elizabeth woodville's signature

Henry VII

(Society of Artiquaries of London)

CHAPTER TWENTY ONE

"... then, in a moment see
How soon this mightiness meets misery,
And if you can be merry then, I'll say
A man may weep upon his wedding-day."
[Henry VIII]

The most celebrated continuation of the blood-line of Elizabeth Woodville was through her eldest daughter, Elizabeth of York, wife to Henry Tudor and ancestress thereby of every monarch to sit on England's throne for the next five and more centuries. However, within less than 50 years of the death of the Queen-dowager, was born another girl, great-granddaughter to Elizabeth Woodville whose manipulation as an instrument of others' overweening ambition almost ended the continuing link with the ancient House of Plantagenet. The child's name was Jane Grey.

Thomas Grey, Marquess of Dorset, step-son of Edward IV and eldest child of Elizabeth Woodville had two marriages arranged for him by his ambitious mother. The first, to Anne Holland, heiress to the Exeter Dukedom had failed on the death of the child-bride, the second to Cicely Bonville had been a more successful union and produced a male heir to the Dorset line, again named Thomas, who inherited the title while in his late teens in August 1501. The second Marquess married Margaret Wotton and, comparatively late in life, a son was born to him and called Henry, after the vigorous young monarch, eighth of that name, who ruled all England.

King Henry VIII was the only survivor of the four sons born to Elizabeth of York and his sisters were scarcely more fortunate, since only two of four survived to womanhood. Margaret, nearly two years older than Henry, married James IV of Scotland who, with the flower of his chivalry, died at Flodden Field. She then married Archibald Douglas, Earl of Angus and, was thereby, grandmother both to Mary, Queen of Scots and Henry, Lord Darnley and great-grandam, therefore, on both sides to James I of England and VI of Scotland.

Henry's sister Mary was five years younger than he and was

undoubtedly his favourite. Vivacious and beautiful, she was betrothed at 19 to the much-older King Louis XII of France and married to him in October 1514. Predictably, perhaps, Louis was dead by New Year's Eve leaving Mary free to re-marry, subject only to the will and whims of the King, her brother. Before her marriage, Mary had formed a strong attachment to Charles Brandon, Duke of Suffolk and bosom friend of King Henry. Brandon had been brought up with the royal children since his father, William Brandon, had carried Henry Tudor's standard at Bosworth and died under the last charge of England's last Plantaganet King, and the debt of blood had been honoured.

Charles Brandon was cast in the same mould as one of the forgotten forebears of the royal Tudors, Richard Woodville. He was big, handsome, not very bright and - again similarly - was raised by sheer good fortune, to a station in life which he was not really capable of filling. He was totally loyal to the King who had ennobled him and had been sent by Henry to France to represent England at Mary's coronation in the November following her marriage. It was natural, therefore, though perhaps less than wise, that he should be sent to France again in January 1515 leading the escort sent to bring the widowed Queen-dowager of France home to England.

Mary Tudor was a lovely and head-strong Princess who was determined that, this time, her marriage would be as she had planned it and, with the active collusion of Francis I, the new King of France, who was quite happy to see Louis' widow neutralised through marriage with an English milord, she and Brandon married secretly in February. The parallel with the secret bonding of Jacquetta of Luxembourg and Richard Woodville continued when the happy couple had to concoct a letter to the King's chief counsellor, Thomas Wolsey, explaining their dilemma in light of the bride's probable pregnancy. And again, forgiveness was forthcoming - at a price: the return of Mary's dowry to her brother and surrender of all plate and jewellery "acquired" by the Queen-dowager as a result of her brief first marriage. In all, the price of filial forgiveness came in at around £40,000 - Bluff King Hal was, indeed, a true son of Henry Tudor.

Mary and Brandon were "married" in public at Greenwich on May 13th 1515 and their first child, a son, was born on March 11th of the year following. A year later still, Mary had the first of two daughters who was christened Frances and who, in due time, would re-make the blood link between Woodvilles and Greys, through marriage with Henry Grey, third Marquess of Dorset and, eventually, in right of his wife, Duke of Suffolk. It

Mary Tudor and Charles Brandon

(Wedding portrait by Jan Mabuse)

was a joining which would again bring disaster to the families - to Dorset, to his first-born, and to other men whose ambition, in the end, outweighed their ability.

Henry VIII died in the early morning of January 28th, 1547 leaving one legitimate son, Edward, who succeeded to the crown as sixth King of that name at the age of nine years and three months. He was the only child of the union between Henry and his third Queen, Jane Seymour and, during his legal infancy, his rule according to his father's Will, was to be governed by a council of sixteen executors, all with equal power. The impracticality of such an arrangement became clear within days of King Henry's death and the council effectively voted itself out of existence and its replacement by a Lord Protector for which post the most suitable candidate was the young King's uncle, Edward Seymour, Earl of Hertford. King Edward, during his father's last days, had been residing at Hertford's castle and, on his appointment as Protector, the Earl wasted no time in bringing the King to London where, on January 31st, he was greatly welcomed by his people.

On February 18th, Edward Seymour became Duke of Somerset to emphasise his new status as Lord Protector and his younger brother, Thomas, was created Baron Seymour of Sudeley. Another to be further ennobled, at the same time, was John Dudley, Lord Lisle, who was made Earl of Warwick, a title singularly appropriate for a man of enormous ambition whose private agenda included, eventually, the making of Kings. The following day, the young King rode through cheering crowds, his uncle by his side, and was duly crowned at Westminster Abbey. When the ceremonials were completed, Edward VI returned to his schooling, leaving the serious business of Government in the hands of his uncle, Edward Seymour, Duke of Somerset.

Thomas Seymour had hoped for greater things than a Barony from the accession of his nephew, and the office of Lord High Admiral handed on to him by John Dudley who now had bigger fish to fry and, when it appeared that his older brother felt quite capable of running England's affairs without filial assistance, he decided to find another way to place his own grasp on the reins of power. Before her marriage to King Henry, Katherine Parr, his sixth and last Queen, had been courted by Seymour and now, as Queen-dowager, independently wealthy and, at 34, still comparatively young and attractive, she made an alluring target for her former swain who had remained unmarried and was now approaching forty years of age. There were two further attractions: living with Queen Katherine were Elizabeth, King Henry's second daughter and Jane Grey, granddaughter of the late King's favourite sister Mary, Duchess of Suffolk.

Seymour and Queen Katherine married secretly in the Spring of 1547. The bride had been somewhat reluctant to disregard the normal period of mourning required of a widow, but, when Thomas Seymour easily secured the approval of his nephew, Edward VI, for the match, the union went ahead. Once the couple had openly taken up residence together, there soon followed talk of early morning frolics involving Katherine's step-daughter, the Princess Elizabeth, then just past 14 years of age. The Queen-dowager apparently gave little weight to such rumours, but afterwards made a point of being with her new husband when he set off for his bedroom romps, which, he had assured her, were solely the kind of game any father would play to get his daughter out of bed betimes.

Katherine's second long-term guest, Jane Grey, great-great granddaughter of Elizabeth Woodville, was younger than her cousin Elizabeth, quieter, and with an almost frightening dedication to education. At little more than 10 years of age she was extending her already formidable learning to include French, Greek and Italian and seems to have had little difficulty keeping pace with her older cousins in the schoolroom. In brief, she was a book-worm. Today, in all probability, she would be termed a swot. Be that as it may, by the terms of her uncle Henry's will, in the event of his own line - Edward, Mary and Elizabeth - failing, the succession would pass to the descendants of his younger sister Mary and, with the death of her brother 13 years earlier, that made Frances Brandon, Duchess of Suffolk, fourth in line followed immediately by her daughter, the young, highly-intelligent Lady Jane Grey.

Jane did not get on at all well with her parents, who, in many ways, were an exact reduplication of the founding couple of Henry Grey's noble line, Jacquetta of Luxembourg and Richard Woodville. Frances was a strong, horsey woman, very conscious of her royal descent, lively, vigorous, ebullient even, while her husband was handsome, persuasive, impecunious despite his title, and ambitious beyond his mental capacity. It was a combination of the last two characteristics which led him to sell the right to arrangement of Jane's marriage and, effectively, her guardianship, to his new friend, Thomas

Seymour, uncle to the King and quite capable, he had indicated, of renewing the marital ties between the House of Grey and the ruler of England. Once such a desirable match had been consummated, then some rearrangement of priorities would be in order, but, for the moment, the Marquis of Dorset was happy to let matters develop.

One year later, the world had turned upside down. In the Autumn and early Winter of 1547, a serious rift had arisen and grown between the Seymours. Thomas had tried to persuade the King to support a petition to the first Parliament of the new reign, separating the Offices of Lord Protector and Governor of the King's Household with the latter responsibility being filled by Lord Thomas. His hopes of gaining possession of the king's person thereby were thwarted by the Protector and, after a period of black rages, sulking fits and open hostility towards Somerset, Thomas Seymour saw there was nothing to be gained in this way and became, apparently, reconciled to his brother.

In the Spring of the following year, Queen Katherine had begun to experience a difficult first pregnancy, hardly surprising for a woman of her age, and she felt it would be better for her health to retire to her husband's estate at Sudeley in Gloucestershire. Jane Grey went with them when they set out on June 13th, but the Princess Elizabeth, for whatever reason, went to stay with family friends at Cheshunt. Three months later, Queen Katherine, having given birth to a healthy girl, died of post-natal fever and was buried in the chapel at Sudeley.

Lord Seymour was undoubtedly badly affected by this personal tragedy and sent Lady Jane home to her parents while he tried to get his affairs in order. Soon however, his customary ebullience returned and he regained possession of Jane by means of further payments and assurances to her perennially hard-up father. In addition, he began to pay suit to Elizabeth and continued to press his courtship on her disregarding advice to the contrary from friends and others less well-disposed. In the latter category was his former friend, John Dudley, Earl of Warwick, who had long awaited his opportunity to set the Seymours at each other's throats and now seized his chance eagerly.

Thomas Seymour was arrested on January 17th, 1549 by order of the Protector and the King's Council and, although his disposal was delayed by

Lady Jane Grey, the Nine Days Queen.

(Geoffrey Wheeler)

Warwick's lengthy, and unsuccessful, efforts to involve Elizabeth in Seymour's alleged plots, he was condemned through a Bill of Attainder which, on 24th February, was approved by the Council and confirmed by the Protector and the young King. This method of condemning a traitor did away with any necessity for the potentially embarrassing public trial, which Seymour had demanded, and he was executed at the Tower a month later.

Protector Somerset, feeling his position weakened by his brother's disgrace and execution, became progressively suspicious and intolerant of any opposition to his policies within the King's Council. This unpopular, dictatorial attitude was cleverly encouraged by Warwick, who felt that his own opportunity to grasp the supreme power held by his predecessor in the title a century earlier was nearly come, and was making final adjustments to his plans. Among these, a prime concern was the destiny of Lady Jane Grey, through whose claim to the crown the status of the Dudley family might be improved from nobility to virtual royalty.

Protector Somerset

(Detail from Traditional Portrait)

CHAPTER TWENTY TWO

"...Last scene of all, That ends this strange eventful history..."
[As You Like It]

The year 1549 was a troubled one for England. Prices were rising as was unemployment and the massive changes made by Henry VIII in the country's religious system left the people without local spiritual comfort to turn to; the Abbeys were gone and with them the saving charity they had dispensed in times of distress. In June, the Protector proclaimed that the Anti-Enclosure laws must be strictly enforced to prevent the landowners turning people out of their homes and smallholdings, but the magnates ignored this and continued their profitable policy of turning arable land into wide sheep-grazing pastures. Soon there were reports of risings in the western counties and in East Anglia and the great houses and estates felt the effects of the people's wrath through looting and burning. Somerset, whose basic policies had made him "the people's Duke", did little to quell the unrest and the Council turned instead to Warwick. John Dudley knew his hour had come.

Marching northeast out of London at the head of a strong well-armed force, Warwick moved decisively against the main body of Norfolk rebels led by a tanner called Robert Ket. On August 24th, now leading an army nearly 8,000 strong, he thrust into Norwich, second city of the kingdom, and drove the rebels' force which had been occupying it back to their headquarters on Mousehold Heath. Two days later, having reports that the rebels had fired their encampment and were moving away towards Dussindale, Warwick marched speedily in pursuit, taking with him only his heavy cavalry and 1,200 German mercenary infantry. He came up with the rebels at Dussindale, which a local "seer" had prophesied would soon be "filled with slaughtered bodies" and after a peremptory offer of quarter - which, predictably, was refused - his army charged the ill-armed, undisciplined mass of peasants and quickly reduced them to a fleeing rabble. Over 3,000 bodies were scattered across Dussindale in fulfilment of the prophecy; the Norfolk rebellion was at an end.

Robert Ket and his brother William escaped the disaster but were captured within days and taken to Norwich to witness the execution by hanging of 150 captured rebels. The two were sent to London for a show trial and both were condemned to death by hanging. The sentences were carried out on December 7th, Robert dying in Norwich Castle, his brother - more spectacularly - being suspended from Wymondham steeple. Two months earlier, Edward Seymour, Duke of Somerset and Lord Protector had found himself a prisoner in the Tower. Under increasing pressure from Warwick, Seymour had made a dramatic flight to Windsor Castle, taking the boy King with him and sending out proclamations to rally support. This had not been forthcoming and on October 10th, Somerset meekly surrendered his charge. In the following Council meeting, the Office of Lord Protector was permanently abolished. The Council had a new leader and King Edward a new mentor, John Dudley, Earl of Warwick and, in light of his new dignities, soon to be Duke of Northumberland.

John Dudley's father, Edmund, was a commoner who had stood high in the favour of Henry VII, since he was a skilled gatherer-in of taxes, but he had been framed on treason charges and was executed by Henry VIII shortly after his accession. However, this set-back simply made an already determined, ambitious, and highly intelligent young man, doubly resolved to succeed and he quickly drew the favourable attention of the new King and rose swiftly in Henry's service as soldier/diplomat, being created first Lord Lisle and then Earl of Warwick. With Somerset removed from the court scene, Dudley exercised all his charm and diplomacy to secure the trust and friendship of King Edward and, as usual, was successful. In the Summer of 1550, an Embassy arrived from Paris to conclude a new Anglo-French Treaty and they were received magnificently with the solemnity of the necessary State functions continuously relieved by feasts, bear-baiting, jousting and firework displays, all of which were thoroughly enjoyed by the young monarch.

In the Autumn of the following year, Mary of Guise, Queen-Regent of Scotland passed through England, en route home from a visit to her daughter in France, and a great State banquet was held in her honour at Westminster. Among the guests invited were Henry Grey and his wife Frances, now Duke and Duchess of Suffolk through the deaths from sickness of Frances's half-brothers, together with their daughter, Lady Jane Grey. Perhaps Henry Grey's new dignity gave rise to a further surge in Dudley's ambitions, or it may be that the King wished to reward his much-liked mentor, whatever the reason, the Earl of Warwick became Duke of Northumberland at that time, the first descendant of a commoner family to attain such high rank. To strengthen his position still further, the new Duke trumped up charges of treason against Somerset, who had recently been restored to membership of the Council, on which he was tried at the beginning of December, found guilty and executed.

In the Spring of 1552, the King's health started to give cause for concern and, within a year, it became clear that he was dying of tuberculosis. Dudley, realising that his own position would become precarious with the loss of his royal sponsor, had taken soundings with the Princesses, Mary and Elizabeth. Unfortunately for him, he found Mary had a long memory and had bitterly resented the estrangement from her brother, of which she [rightly] regarded Dudley as prime architect, because she refused to renounce her Catholic faith. Elizabeth, with her own memories of her alleged involvement in Seymour's plotting and the jeopardy this had put her in, would have no truck with any approaches made by the Duke. He was therefore obliged to play the last trump card left to him. Towards the end of May 1553, his fifth and only unmarried son, Lord Guildford Dudley, became the husband of Lady Jane Grey.

On July 6th, Edward, only legitimate son of Henry VIII and third Tudor monarch of England, died - a merciful release from a disease-ridden and pain-racked body - but, before his end, he had made his Will, which included what he called his Device for the Succession. The main effect of this document was to exclude his sisters, Mary and Elizabeth, from succeeding to the throne and to pass over Frances Brandon, Duchess of Suffolk, the next in line, in favour of her daughter Jane. On the sixth of July, 1553 therefore, due in large measure to his own planning and clever opportunism, John Dudley, Earl of Warwick, Duke of Northumberland, son of a commoner executed for treason, became father-in-law to the Queen of England. Triumph indeed, but one which for him and even more unhappily for the descendant of Elizabeth Woodville, first of her house to rule in England, would be short-lived and eventually lethal.

With Edward's death, it was time for Dudley to put the final phase of his scheme into effect. To succeed, it was essential for him to have custody of the King's sisters, Mary and Elizabeth, and to this end, he kept Edward's demise secret and sent urgently to the two Princesses that their brother was on his death-bed and had asked for their presence. Elizabeth smelled a rat and sent back that she herself was sick and would come as soon as she had recovered, but Mary, ever more credulous than her sister, replied that she would be with her brother as soon as she could and set out immediately from Hunsdon on the short journey south. Fortunately for her, she had travelled only a few miles when she received a message from Nicholas Throckmorton, a servant of her brother, advising her that the King was dead and the call for her presence at his bedside, a trap. She immediately turned eastwards, making for Kenninghall in Norfolk, where she knew she would find sure refuge and an easy path to the coast should further flight be needed.

After a fruitless wait of three days, Dudley decided that urgent action was required and he despatched his son, Lord Robert Dudley, with a strong mounted escort and orders to find and arrest the Princess Mary and take her to the Tower. Lady Jane was requested to attend a gathering at Syon House where she was waited on by Northumberland in his capacity as leader of the Council and the Lords of this inner Cabinet, together with her parents, her mother-in-law and her husband of six weeks. The gathering was to hear the formal announcement of King Edward's death and his handing-on of the supreme royal power to his cousin Lady Jane Grey.

The following day, Queen Jane travelled in the state barge to her new residence in the Tower and heralds went about the city proclaiming her to be England's new ruler, an announcement which was generally received in sullen silence. For Londoners at least, the true heir was undoubtedly Princess Mary and they were far from happy to have the unknown wife of one of the hated Dudleys foisted on them as their new Queen. Within the Tower, there was equally little accord, particularly when Jane made it clear that Guildford, as a commoner, could not possibly become King of England. She would give him a dukedom and with that distinction he and his family must rest content. The boy sulked, the mother-in-law raged, but all to no purpose, Jane Grey was a determined little girl, however small of stature she might be.

Late in the same day, a formal letter to the royal Council arrived, written by Princess Mary, now moved to the strong fortress of Framlingham, from where she required them to recognise her immediately as their Queen and to proclaim her right to succeed and her title to the throne throughout the capital. With this demand, came news of nobles and gentlemen moving towards Norfolk seemingly rallying to Mary's support and a report that Norwich was supplying men and arms to her cause. Clearly drastic counter-action had to be taken and Dudley immediately sent out orders for a mustering of troops which would leave for Norfolk on July 13th to arrest the recalcitrant Princess and disperse her forces. The royal army would be led by Queen Jane's father, Henry Grey, Duke of Suffolk.

This last stipulation caused consternation in Council and to the new Queen. Henry Grey, like all his family before him, may have cut a pretty figure in the tiltyard, but he was not - nor, to do him justice, did he pretend to be - a man of war. So, when the Queen attended the Council in tears begging them not to give this perilous commission to her father, there was little argument and, instead, the Duke of Northumberland, whose success against the Ket rebels was still fresh in mind, was asked to take command of the expedition. Grudgingly, John Dudley agreed. He knew well that it was vital to keep a tight grip on London if his hold on power was to be maintained, and he doubted the ability and, in some cases, the willingness of his noble colleagues to hold the capital for Queen Jane. But, he was an intelligent and experienced statesman and general and perhaps could see that his only throw left was to eliminate Princess Mary. So, early in the morning of July 14th 1553, like Richard, last Plantagenet King, in similar case, he gathered his cavalry and set out on one last wild ride - Caesar or nothing.

Almost as soon as Northumberland, riding through sullen hostile crowds, was beyond the city gates, the reign of Queen Jane began to crumble. There was no longer a strong hand controlling London. As the people increasingly filled all the streets, the royal Council dithered and delayed, the Queen too young, her father too weak to stem the flowing tide of sentiment, which was fed continuously by a stream of reports of desertions from Northumberland's army. And, in the evening of July 19th, at the Cross in Cheapside, Mary Tudor was proclaimed Queen by her rejoicing people. Henry Grey, Duke of Suffolk, carried the news to his daughter at the Tower then, pausing only on Tower Hill to proclaim formally that Mary Tudor was Queen of England, Grey fled to Sheen Palace, leaving his daughter alone in the empty rooms of state to await her ruler's judgement.

The reign of the only Woodville ever to be ruler of England had lasted nine days.

Epilogue

"... last of the Popinjays ..."

Queen Mary Tudor, who would go down in England's annals as Bloody Mary after a six year reign of religious intolerance, involving public burnings and executions, and arguably the most unpopular marriage ever made by a British monarch, started her rule in a gentle and forgiving manner. Jane Grey was given pleasant quarters looking on to Tower Green with servants and a page to wait on her and Mary constantly rejected the advice of her closest counsellors that she should be executed. For John Dudley, lately Earl of Warwick and Duke of Northumberland, there could be no such mercy and he went to his death, together with two of his henchmen, on the 21st of August.

Henry Grey, Duke of Suffolk, made his submission to the new Queen and was given his liberty and kept his estates. Six months later, this weak, silly man was engaged in trying to raise the Midlands in support of a rebellion led by Sir Thomas Wyatt, who was leading 5,000 Kentish men towards London to prevent the Queen's intended marriage with Philip of Spain. For a while the rebel army was successful and many royal troops deserted to its ranks as it neared London. On February 1st, 1554, Wyatt stood on the brink of success, having reached the outskirts and started his men pushing forward through Southwark towards the inner city, but he was halted by Mary's brave action in addressing the Lord Mayor and Aldermen, and her people, urging her cause and when Wyatt reached London Bridge, he found it barred against him. Backtracking to Kingston he crossed the river there days later and tried to advance again, but his army was discouraged by the setback, cold and hungry and, finding itself now progressively opposed in its advance, began to melt away until only Wyatt with a few close supporters was left. They surrendered at Temple Bar and on February 7th were imprisoned in the Tower.

Whilst the rebels, Wyatt and her father, had to wait for their justice, their rebellion brought a swifter end to the 16 year old Jane Grey and her husband, Guildford Dudley. Frightened by the resurgence of Protestant dissent and angered by the base ingratitude of Henry Grey, the Queen hesitated no longer to sign the death warrants when her advisers brought them to her and, on February 12th, Guildford Dudley was publicly beheaded on Tower Hill. Jane Grey as a Princess of the royal blood was despatched privately, immediately afterwards on the Green outside her quarters, attended by the Abbot of Westminster, Feckenham, and her maids, Nurse Ellen and Mrs Tilney.

In the following month, Sir Thomas Wyatt, after painful questioning aimed - unsuccessfully - at implicating the Princess Elizabeth in the rebellion's planning, paid the due penalty for his treason.

Henry Grey, Duke of Suffolk, most typical descendant of Jacquetta of Luxembourg and Richard Woodville - fop, wastrel, last of the Popinjays - died with him.

John Dudley, Duke of Northumberland

(Detail from Traditional Portrait)

ACKNOWLEDGEMENTS

The world of Students of History covers the globe and, at the same time, is a very small parish, nowadays made smaller yet by the Internet.

This makes it easy to bridge vast distances in no time at all and to "converse" with people with similar interests on a continuing - sometimes 'continuous' would be a more accurate description - basis. It is simple therefore to call upon friendly correspondents for instant confirmation of facts and to discuss, more generally, historical matters of immediate or impending interest.

I have used this facility extensively in researching and writing "The Popinjays", as have my correspondents, whose dwellings are as far apart as California and New South Wales, with some much closer to hand - a mere 150 or 200 miles away from my home - in the land of my birth.

In summary, therefore, this book is the product of many more brains than my own, united through the Internet and the World Wide Web and it is time to thank them for their support and encouragement and help, without which - as they say - this, the first-ever History of the Woodville family, would not have been written.

So, heartfelt and most sincere thanks to :

— my dear friend, Judy Pimental [who may NOT be called 'Judith'] of Alameda, California - and currently serving in the Peace Corps for the good of others - for the gift of her own notes on [and a copy of] the biography of Elizabeth Woodville, which gave me a starting point. -

— my lovely niece, Brenda Skogg, of Ocean Shores, New South Wales, who loves ferreting about down the mouseholes of the World Wide Web and continually comes up with the detail I have been unsuccessfully digging for everywhere else, including the ancestry of Lady Jane Grey -

— Geoffrey Wheeler, Keeper of the pictorial archives of the Richard III Society and adviser, sans egal, on all matters-illustrative relating to the English Medieval Age. His expertise in this field continues to astonish me -

— The Society of Antiquaries of London for permission to use the royal portraits from their collection and particularly to their Assistant Librarian, Adrian James for his prompt and courteous responses to my requests -

— and, last but far from least, to my friend and fellow-Ricardian Christine Symonds, Librarian of the Yorkshire Branch of the Richard III Society, whose ever-ready help in supplying source material has to be experienced to be properly appreciated.

SOURCES

The invaluable, initial source for The Popinjays was the biography by David MacGibbon, "Elizabeth Woodville, her life and times" published by Arthur Barker of London in 1938. Unfortunately, his views on many of the Queen's actions and motives differ widely from my own and his adherence to the "traditional" view of the fate of the Princes in the Tower is totally at variance with my own beliefs, so that it became progressively necessary to re-delve into other authorities as the writing progressed. However, it would be churlish not to acknowledge MacGibbon's helpfulness in the early stages.

The "other authorities" on the medieval period which I consulted frequently are the Crowland Chronicle [second continuation]; The Usurpation of Richard III [Mancini/Armstrong]: Henry VII [Bacon/Lumby]; Richard III by Paul Murray Kendall and books on the Tudor dynasty [NOT my favourite period] by Alison Plowden and Josephine Ross

In addition I found helpful and/or confirmatory excerpts in Black's English History, Warkworth, Bentley, Burne and in a short essay on Elizabeth Woodville's funeral by Sutton and Visser-Fuchs in The Ricardian, March 1999.

Much minor detail is culled from my own voluminous, badly-filed and occasionally indecipherable notes, which have been amassed over many years' casual research and reading and which, unhappily, all too seldom refer to the original source from which they came. If I have inadvertently, therefore, omitted to mention the source of what readers may find to be useful - even valuable - information within The Popinjays, I can only offer my profound apologies for my poor recording skills and for not, on occasions, being able to decipher my own ancient handscript.

Index

ANJOU, Margaret of, Queen of
Henry VI   15, 19, 24/27, 29, 35,
      37/8, 41, 53/4, 65/6, 71, 75, 86

AUDLEY. James Touchet, Lord   29/30

BEAUFORT, Edmund, 1st Duke
of Somerset   25/26, 97

BEAUFORT, Henry, 2nd Duke of
Somerset   15, 17, 19, 27, 30/32, 37, 41

BEAUFORT, Edmund, 3rd Duke
of Somerset   75

BEAUFORT, Margaret, Countess of
Richmond, [Mother of Henry Tudor]   86, 95/101,
      103/04, 110/11, 113/16, 120/21,
      123/24, 126

BEDFORD, John, Duke of, [brother to
Henry V] [First husband to Jacquetta of
Luxembourg]   21/2, 24, 46

BRANDON, Charles, Duke of Suffolk,   130

BRANDON, Frances [d. of Mary Tudor
and Charles Brandon]   130, 133, 138

BRAY, Reginald, [Steward to
Margaret Beaufort]   100, 105, 120/21

BUCKINGHAM, Humphrey Stafford,
1st Duke of,   25, 35/6

BUCKINGHAM, Henry Stafford,
2nd Duke of,   46, 83, 93/4, 97/100, 102/05,
      107/10, 113/16

BURGH, Sir Thomas,   62/3

BURGUNDY, Charles, Duke of,   51, 69, 71/2, 81

BUTLER, Lady Eleanor,   98, 101, 121

CATESBY, William,   89, 99, 115, 120

CLAPHAM, John of Skipton, Captain,   57/58

CLARENCE, George, Duke of,   45, 49/51,
      53, 56, 62/6, 73, 75, 79/85

CLIFFORD, John, Lord,
["Bloody Clifford"]   15/17, 27, 37

CLIFFORD, Thomas, Lord,
[Father of John]   25/26

CONYERS, Sir John,   58, 63/64

DACRE, Thomas, Lord,   15, 18/19

DEVON, Thomas Courtenay, Earl of,   15, 37

DEVON, Henry Courtenay, Earl of,   52

DUDLEY, John, Lord,   29/30

DUDLEY, John, Earl of Warwick,
[Later Duke of Northumberland]   132, 134,
      136/142

DUDLEY, Guildford, Lord,
[Husband of Lady Jane Grey]   139/140, 142/43

DYNHAM, John, Sea-captain,   31/32

EDWARD IV,   15/20, 22, 31, 33,
      35/6, 38/43, 46/7, 49/53, 55/66,
      68/9, 71/89, 91/2, 94, 96/8, 101, 103,
      108, 116, 118, 121, 124, 127.

EDWARD, Prince of Wales,
[Later Edward V]   70, 77/8, 88/9, 91/2,
      94/5, 98, 101/02, 104/05,
      107/11, 113, 116, 126

EDWARD of Lancaster, Prince of Wales,
[Son of Henry VI]   27, 35, 37, 65, 71, 75, 77

EDWARD of Middleham, Prince
of Wales, [Son of Richard III]   119

EDWARD VI [Only son of
Henry VIII]   132/34, 136, 138/140

ELIZABETH of York, Queen to
Henry VII, [daughter of Edward IV]   47, 61, 65,
      80, 86, 88, 103/04, 118/120, 123/26, 129.

ELIZABETH Tudor,
[Later Elizabeth I]   133/34, 136, 139, 140, 143

EXETER, Henry Holland, Duke of,   73/74

GREY, Frances, Duchess of
Suffolk, [See under BRANDON, Frances]

GREY, Henry, 3rd Marquess of
Dorset, [Later Duke of Suffolk]   129/130,
      132/34, 138, 141/43

GREY, Lady Jane, The Nine-days
Queen,   129, 132/34 136, 138, 140/43

GREY, Sir John, Lord Ferrers
of Groby, [First husband of
Elizabeth Woodville]   20, 27, 29, 38/39

GREY, Richard, Lord
[Stepson of Edward IV]   39/40, 79, 88,
                                91/93, 101/02
GREY, Thomas, 1st Marquess of
Dorset, [Stepson of Edward IV]   27, 40, 48,
                79, 84, 88, 91, 93, 95, 102/03,
                        113, 116, 124, 128/29
GREY, Thomas, 2nd Marquess of Dorset,   129
GRUTHUYSE, Louis de, Governor
of Holland.   69, 78
HASTINGS, William, Lord,   41, 60, 68,
                    72, 74/5, 79, 89, 91,
                    93/101, 109, 115, 121
HENRY VI,   15, 21/24, 27, 29, 31,
                    33, 35/7, 39, 41, 47, 66,
                    69, 76/7, 83,
HENRY VII   95/96, 100, 103/04,
                110/11. 113/16, 118, 120/26,
                        129/130, 138
HENRY VIII   127, 129/130, 132, 137/39
HERBERT, Sir William, later Lord,
[Briefly, Earl of Pembroke]   40, 52, 57/59, 61
JAMES III, King of Scotland,   85, 87, 118, 126
JACQUETTA of Luxembourg,
Duchess of Bedford, [Wife to
Sir Richard Woodville]   22, 24, 26/7,
                39/42, 45/6, 50/1, 54, 58/9, 61,
                69, 77/8, 82, 127, 130, 133, 143
KET, Robert & William,
Norfolk Rebel Leaders,   137/38,141
LOUIS XI, King of France,   43, 47, 50, 62,
                64/6, 71/2, 75, 80, 83, 85/6,
                        104, 110, 113
LOVELL, Francis, Viscount,   125/26
LUXEMBOURG, Jean de, Uncle
to Jacquetta,   45
LUXEMBOURG, Jacques de,
Brother to Jacquetta,   46, 50
MARGARET of York,
Duchess of Burgundy,   51/2, 55, 68, 81/2, 125
MARGARET Tudor, Queen
of Scotland. [Sister to Henry VIII]   129

MARY Tudor, Queen of France,
later Duchess of Suffolk
[Sister to Henry VIII]   129/130, 133
MARY Tudor, [Later Mary I]   139/142
MORTON, John, Bishop of Ely,
later Cardinal/Archbishop of
Canterbury,   80, 96/100, 103/05,
            108, 110/11, 113/16, 123, 125/26
NEVILLE, Anne, daughter of
Warwick, [Later Queen of
Richard III]   49, 66, 77, 81, 103, 119/120
NEVILLE, Cecily, Duchess of
York,   20, 31, 68, 73, 86, 102
NEVILLE, George, Archbishop
of York, [Brother of Warwick],   45, 47, 52, 56, 58
NEVILLE, Isabel, daughter of
Warwick, [Later Duchess of Clarence]   49. 51,
                                56. 80/1. 119
NEVILLE, John, Lord [of Raby]   15, 18
NEVILLE, John, Lord [later
Marquess] Montagu,   40/42, 47, 55,
                        60/1, 68, 72/4, 79
NEVILLE, Richard, Earl of
Salisbury,   27, 29/32, 35, 37/8, 47
NEVILLE, Richard, Earl of Warwick,
["Warwick the Kingmaker"]   16, 26/7, 29/33,
                        35/8, 40/3, 45/56, 58/66,
                        68/74, 81/2, 92, 119
NEVILLE, William, Lord
Fauconberg, [Later Earl of Kent] 17, 31, 33, 35, 41
NORFOLK, John Mowbray, Duke of,   17, 19
NORFOLK, John Howard, Duke of,   103, 114
NORTHUMBERLAND, Henry
Percy, 3rd Earl of,   15, 18
NORTHUMBERLAND, Henry
Percy, 4th Earl of,   29, 37, 61/2, 72, 102, 123
OGLE, Sir Robert, later Lord,   56/57
OXFORD, John de Vere, Earl of,   46, 73/74,
                                121/22, 125
PARR, Katherine, 6th wife of
Henry VIII,   132/34

148

POLE, William de la,
Earl, later Duke, of Suffolk, 21, 24, 25
POLE, John de la, Earl of Lincoln, 125
RATCLIFFE, Richard, 99, 102, 120
RICHARD III, formerly Duke of
Gloucester, 22, 49, 55, 60, 68,
71/5, 77, 81, 85, 87, 89, 91/104,
107/10, 114/16, 118/126, 141
RICHARD of Shrewsbury, Duke
of York, [Younger son of Edward IV] 78, 83,
87/8, 101, 105, 108/11, 116, 126
ROTHERHAM, Thomas, Bishop of
Rochester, [Later, Archbishop of York] 65, 99/100
RUTLAND, Edmund, Earl of, 31. 38
SEYMOUR, Edward, elder brother
of Jane, ["Protector Somerset"] 132/34, 136/39
SEYMOUR' Jane, 3rd wife of Henry
Vl11, [mother of Edward Vl] 132
SEYMOUR, Thomas, younger
brother of Jane, Baron Sudely,
Lord High Admiral, 132/34, 136, 139
SHORE, Jane [Elizabeth] mistress
of Edward IV, [later mistress of
Lord Hastings], 95` 98
SIMNEL, Lambert, Pretender, 125
STANLEY, Thomas, Lord
[later Earl of Derby] [4th husband
of Margaret Beaufort] 95/100, 103,
115, 120/125
STANLEY, Sir William.
brother to Thomas, 121/123
STILLINGTON, Robert, Bishop
of Bath and Wells, [formerly
Chancellor of England] 98
TROLLOPE, Andrew, Captain, 30/33
TUDOR, Henry. See Henry VII.
TUDOR, Jasper, Earl of Pembroke,
[later Duke of Bedford], 37, 52, 75, 121,
124/25, 127
VAUGHAN, Sir Thomas,
tutor to Edward V, 78, 93, 101/02

WARWICK, Richard Neville, Earl of,
See NEVILLE, Richard, Earl of Warwick.
WELLES, Richard, Lord, 62/63
WELLES, Sir Robert, son of
Lord Richard, 62/64
WENLOCK, John, Sea-captain,
later Lord, 32, 53, 55, 64
WILTSHIRE, James Butler, Earl of, 27
WOODVILLE, Elizabeth,
Queen to Edward IV, 20/1, 23, 27,
39/43, 45/50, 53/4, 56/9, 61, 65/6, 68/9,
73/4, 77/83, 85/9, 91/6, 98, 100/104,110/11,
113, 115/16, 119/12O, 124/27, 129, 133, 139
WOODVILLE, SirAnthony, Lord
Scales' [2nd Earl Rivers, brother
to Elizabeth] 32/3,39,52,55/6,59/60,
65, 68, 75, 78, 82, 84/5, 89, 91/4,
101/02, 113
WOODVILLE, Sir Richard,
1st Earl Rivers, [husband of
Jacquetta of Luxembourg] 21/6, 32/3, 39
47, 52/8, 61, 74, 82, 127, 130, 133, 143
WOODVILLE, Richard,
Father of Sir Richard, 21
WOODVILLE Thomas, Lord
of the Manor of Grafton, 21
WOODVILLE Other Siblings
of Elizabeth,
Anne 46
Edward 88, 91, 94/5, 121, 126
John 46, 52, 55/8, 61, 74, 82
Katherine 24, 46, 97
Lionel, Bishop of Salisbury, 86, 91, 113
Margaret 24, 46
Mary 46
Richard 126
WYATT. Sir Thomas, Rebel leader, 142/43
YORK, Richard, Duke of, 16, 21, 23/5, 27,
29, 31, 33, 37/8

Also available from Baildon Books

Geoffrey Richardson's

THE HOLLOW CROWNS

For the first time - all major battles of the Wars of the Roses
in detail and in one volume.

From the fields and gardens by St Albans on an early Summer's day in
1455, to the death of the last Plantagenet King of England, alone, betrayed
and hopelessly mired in marshland below Bosworth's Ambion Hill, the reader
is swept along through three decades of English History.

Encountering along the way: the hapless Henry VI, pathetic son of the
victor of Agincourt; Margaret of Anjou, Henry's Queen and Lancaster's
champion for 20 years; Richard Neville, fabled Kingmaker Warwick, who -
the story shows - has enjoyed a greater reputation in history than his deeds
warranted; the giant Edward IV, England's greatest Warrior-King, and
Richard, his youngest brother, arguably the last true monarch of England and
almost certainly the worst-slandered.

This all-new account of the bloodiest 30 years in English History has
been termed: "History made easy - and interesting!" Written in a fresh
narrative style, with full-page, "3D" Battlemaps of all eleven major conflicts
and portraits of the principal participants (including line-drawings of Warwick
and Margaret of Anjou developed from computer-enhanced sources) "THE
HOLLOW CROWNS" puts the story back into History.

ISBN 0 9527621 0 2

£5.99

AND...

Geoffrey Richardson's

"THE DECEIVERS"

This History covers the last two years of the internecine struggle between York and Lancaster - the so-called Wars of the Roses - from the death of Edward IV in April 1483, to the defeat and death of his successor, Richard III, at Bosworth, and through the early years of the usurper, Henry Tudor, to the end of the 15th Century.

Written in this author's easy narrative style, "The Deceivers" sets out to answer four main questions :

- *Why was the life of William, Lord Hastings ended so abruptly and ingloriously by his former comrade-in-arms -*

- *Why should Henry Stafford, second Duke of Buckingham, rebel against the King he had helped to his throne three months earlier -*

- *How could a seasoned warrior like Richard III lose the Battle of Bosworth against what was, at best, a "rabble in arms" -*

and, most important of all,

- *Who killed the Princes in the Tower, and When, and Why -*

The answers to all these questions are set down in "The Deceivers" and reveal a stunning conspiracy on the part of a handful of people, who have never previously been indicted for the crimes of which they are guilty, but who changed the course of English History.

ISBN 09527621 1 0

£5.99

AND...

Geoffrey Richardson's

"THE LORDLY ONES"

The original History of the Neville family, from its beginnings in the reign of King John, to its effective end in the swirling mists of Barnet on Easter Day, 1471.

From their great Keep at Middleham and their other northern fortresses at Barnard, Sheriff Hutton, Carlisle and Richmond, the Nevilles spread their power throughout England, notably through Richard Neville, Earl of Warwick, who made another power-base at Warwick Castle and sought to rule all the land by the making and unmaking of Kings.

The saga of his efforts - and his failure - is an important element in this history, but the author, in his inimitable, easy-read style, shows that there was much more to the history of the Nevilles than the often-told story of "Warwick the Kingmaker". Among "The Lordly Ones" we meet Ralph Neville, Lord of Raby, victor over the Scots at Nevilles Cross; and another Ralph, first Earl of Westmorland, and most uxorious of all this well-married family, with his brood of 23 children. Joan Beaufort, Ralph's second wife, who brought the blood-royal into the family, with fatal consequences. Cecily Neville, Ralph's youngest, fairest, star-crossed daughter, the Rose of Raby, wife to a would-be King, mother to two more, and Great Grand-dam to the usurping line of Tudors - her greatest tragedy would be to outlive nearly all her line.

And tragedy a-plenty among the other Nevilles: John, Marquis Montagu, the faithful Yorkist, killed fighting for the wrong side. His son George, a royal Duke, heir to the throne of England, who died a pauper dependant on his cousin's charity. And the two daughters of the Kingmaker, who married splendidly - but not wisely - and died young. Not untypically, for death - early and sudden - was the constant attendant of the Lordly Ones, the Nevilles, and of most of those who came close to them.

ISBN 09527621 2 9

£6.99

"THE HOLLOW CROWNS"

"...it is in The Hollow Crowns' vivid descriptions of the wars' 11 major battles that Richardson shows his considerable ability as a researcher and writer. He provides easily understandable explanations of the courses of the battles themselves, displaying an expert knowledge of such decisive factors as topography, weather conditions and weaponry. In addition Richardson presents in an entertaining and comprehensible manner, the complex and highly fluid relationships between the numerous characters involved....As an alternative view of a well-known and turbulent time, The Hollow Crowns is highly recommended to anyone interested in medieval warfare, the history of England, or the foibles of royalty." (MILITARY HISTORY MAGAZINE.)

"THE DECEIVERS"

"...The author, who has been fascinated by history since he was a schoolboy has treated the book as an enthralling detective story... making the subject interesting and entertaining...He makes a persuasive case for Richard III and pins the blame [for the Princes' murder] on the plotting of three 15th century schemers...[He says] I am writing about events that happened 500 years ago, but people were driven then by the same things that drive them now - ambition, pride and desire for power..." (EVENING COURIER)

"THE LORDLY ONES"

"...The pages of The Lordly Ones are full of sex, power and dark deeds in high places, but don't be confused. It is not a modern-day blockbuster. The writer has taken a spin back through the centuries to unearth the story of one of England's most powerful family dynasties and more than 300 years of the Neville family have been retraced in vivid style. The Bradford-based author was asked by English Heritage to write the story of the Nevilles and their Area Director, Sue Constantine said "The book fills an important gap in the story of Middleham Castle and indeed English History generally..." (NORTHERN ECHO)